**Building
a New
Town**

Finland's
New Garden
City

Tapiola

The MIT Press   Cambridge,
Massachusetts,
and London,
England

Building a New Town

Finland's New Garden City

Tapiola

Heikki von Hertzen
and
Paul D. Spreiregen

Copyright © 1971 by The Massachusetts Institute of Technology

This book was designed by Muriel Cooper.
It was set in Fototronic Galaxy by New England Typographic Service, Inc. Printed and bound in the United States of America by The Maple Press Co.

ISBN 0 262 22014 8 (hardcover)

Library of Congress catalog card number: 71–110235

1 The Relevance of Tapiola

2 Background

xi
A Note from the Authors

1
Tapiola in Outline

8
Tapiola in Context

15
New Towns and Garden Cities in History

24
Urbanization, Urbanity, and Urban Form

28
Architectural and Urban Design in Finland

54
Finland's Housing and Planning Programs

68
Facts and Figures

3 Building Tapiola

4 Beyond Tapiola

5 The Lessons of Tapiola

73
Starting

76
**Financing a
Complete Town
from the Beginning**
Site Prices in Tapiola 79
The Financing of the
Housing 80
Financing of the
Municipal Engineering
Costs 82

83
**Programming,
Planning, and
Building**
The First or Eastern
Neighborhood 84
The Town Center 108
The Second or Western
Neighborhood 124
The Third or Northern
Neighborhood 132
Itäranta 146
Tapiola Overall 158

164
**Administration
and Operation**
Tapiola as a
Cross-Section
Community 165
Sales and Marketing 167
Public Information and
Assimilation 169
Service Companies 170

180
**Provocation as a Tool
in Creating a Town**

187
**The Seven Towns
Plan**

198
"Uusimaa 2010"

208
Uusimaa in 1968

215
**A Philosophy for
New Towns**

224
Illustration Credits

225
Index

Family well-being is
not possible without
good housing.

Good housing
is not possible without
good town planning.

Good town planning is
not possible without
good regional planning.

And good regional
planning is not possible
without a national
program for
urbanization.

Heikki von Hertzen

A Note from the Authors

Heikki von Hertzen
Tapiola, Finland

Paul D. Spreiregen
Washington, D.C., U.S.A.

This book is an attempt to produce a complete case study of the creation of a recent new town. It is a collaborative work by two authors, one an outside observer, the other an inside participant, the initiator and leader of the operation. The authors hope that this method combines objectivity and wholeness with authority and accuracy.

The book was prepared over a period of more than two years, starting in the spring of 1967 and reaching completion in the summer of 1969. The authors worked in close collaboration, largely through correspondence but also through several face-to-face work sessions in both Finland and the United States.

Essentially, the "outside" author approached the work as an intense inquiry, investigating from all angles so as to understand what really happened. The "inside" author responded to that inquiry, disclosing the procedure of the whole operation, the creation of the new town, and developing the proper degree of emphasis and detail for the numerous components of the story.

Although both authors shared the entire task of writing, each assumed an appropriate and specific substantive responsibility. The context of the Tapiola story, which forms Chapters 1 and 2, was the duty of the outside author, Paul D. Spreiregen. The Tapiola story itself, which forms Chapters 3 and 4, was the duty of Heikki von Hertzen; for directness and clarity, this portion is told in the first person. The final portion, Chapter 5, was a joint responsibility.

This book is presented in the hope that it will contribute in some measure to the goal of a humane environment for everyone.

**Building
a New
Town**

Finland's
New Garden
City

Tapiola

1 The Relevance of Tapiola

Tapiola in Outline

Tapiola is a new town in Finland whose origins are unique. It was created by a private nonprofit enterprise called Asuntosäätiö (the Housing Foundation), which was established in 1951 by six social and trade organizations. ''We do not want to build houses or dwellings but socially healthful surroundings for contemporary man and his family.'' Thus Tapiola's builders defined their objectives. Their aim was to create a town for everyone, a town in which different social groups could work and live in harmony together.

Asuntosäätiö bought an area of 670 acres in the then-rural county of Espoo outside the city of Helsinki and began planning and building a modern garden city suited to Finnish conditions. The creation of Tapiola meant the building of a whole new urban complex. Asuntosäätiö was not only responsible for the planning, financing, and construction of the dwellings and working places but also for streets, water supply, sewage, street lighting, parks, and public gardens.

Tapiola's planners aimed at demonstrating a new direction for Finnish town planning and housing. They set as their goal the development of a thriving self-contained community. This meant that as many jobs as possible had to be provided—as many as could be at a distance of just six miles from Helsinki. Another basic requirement was that the center of Tapiola be a versatile business, administrative, and cultural focus, satisfying the leisure, cultural, and social demands of the inhabitants as fully as possible.

The starting point for planning was the individuality of man and his proximity to the natural environment. Unpolluted air and safe surroundings with a wide range of choice of activity were basic planning principles. The planners of Tapiola were convinced that no one professional group could solve the manifold problems of modern community planning; planning has to be a highly skilled and strictly directed teamwork at all levels. Tapiola is the result of close teamwork in the fields of architecture, sociology, civil engineering, landscape gardening, domestic science, and child and youth welfare.

In building a modern city in the midst of a rural county, Asuntosäätiö had to solve a series of administrative and financial problems through often farsighted and sometimes extraordinary methods. The number of inhabitants within the inner area of Tapiola as planned and built by Asuntosäätiö is 16,000. In the general plan for the district of Espoo, Tapiola was defined as a ''district center'' serving a maximum population of about 80,000 in Espoo County. As a matter of fact, the population of that county area reached 33,000 by 1967.

Tapiola is neither a rich man's suburb nor a workingman's dormitory. It is a whole town for everyone. The children of blue-collar workers go to school with the children of white-collar workers. Another intention could be realized only in part, that wage earners work in the town itself rather than commute to their jobs. There will be ultimately between five to six thousand jobs in Tapiola. About half of the inhabitants are now employed locally, but that proportion will increase.

Asuntosäätiö enjoyed no special privileges in
realizing its aims. It was in competition for financing and for home buyers in the greater Helsinki market and it competed on those terms.
Financing was by no means easy. Although Tapiola had certain advantages, it enjoyed no special privileges. The site, near the sea, is quite
beautiful and handsomely wooded. In fact the
name "Tapiola" means literally "the realm of
the kingdom of the woods." Bordering the site
of Tapiola is Otaniemi, the locale of the Finnish
Technical Institute, whose creation parallels Tapiola's chronologically. Road access between Tapiola and Helsinki is good, and bus service frequent. Tapiola's real advantages, however, are
its qualities as a modern town. It is in comparison with the features offered by other developments of like nature in or around Helsinki, as
well as by new towns in other countries, that Tapiola's qualities are best judged.

Tapiola Garden City was built as both an experiment and a model. As an experiment, it produced considerable information on how to create
new towns and how to make them socially as
well as economically successful. As a model, it
challenges many accepted ideas on residential
area design and on the future pattern of Finland's urbanization.

On the basis of the Tapiola experience Asuntosäätiö—with an enlarged consortium of development organizations—has embarked on the creation of far larger new towns. It now appears
that the optimum size for an independent town
unit, at least in Southern Finland, would be
about 100,000 inhabitants, in some special
cases possibly 200,000. Asuntosäätiö's work in
the future has been drawn according to these

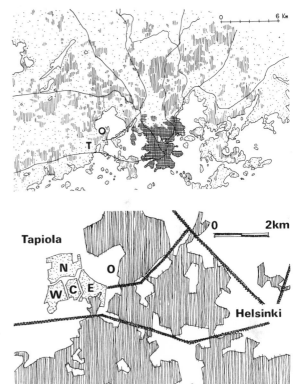

3.
A portion of the Porkkala
site. (foto Atte Matilainen)
4.
A portion of the Espoo site.
(foto Atte Matilainen)

5.
Porkkala (left), Espoo
(center), and Helsinki or
Helsingfors, as it is called in
Swedish. Note the industrial
sectors.
6.
The "Seven Towns Plan,"
1962. Helsinki is the large
circle with 600,000
inhabitants. Just to the left
is the Espoo region where
Tapiola is situated. Next is
Espoo Bay, with 100,000,
and then Porkkala seaside
town, with 200,000. It is
23 miles from Porkkala to
Helsinki. The dots indicate
regional open space.

lines. In that way Asuntosäätiö has been involved in the planning problems of two new
town projects that are known as the Espoo Bay
project and Porkkala Seaside Town. These towns
will also serve all classes of Finland's society,
but they will go much further than Tapiola could
in providing employment for their residents.
While Tapiola is in part a satellite of Helsinki, it
is neither a dormitory nor a nursery. It is a working town with nearly all the attributes of a
town—to the maximum extent that its situation
and the times allowed. The next new towns will
be far more independent operationally. The main
difference between Tapiola and other residential
developments on Helsinki's fringe is that Tapiola
is a whole town; the other developments are primarily dormitories.

Tapiola's principal challenge is to today's typical patterns of urbanization. For most countries
typical pattern means the accelerated growth of
already large cities at the expense of small and
medium size towns and of the rural countryside.
In most cases this growth occurs where there is
an absence of national policy and effective national action to produce alternatives. In most
cases, too, the swelling cities are scarcely capable of managing their growth. This lack of direction is passed on to a city's inhabitants in the
form of inconveniences and burdens that he now
accepts as normal—noise, pollution, poor public
services, transportation bottlenecks, rising taxes,
high land costs, and the shortage of recreation
space.

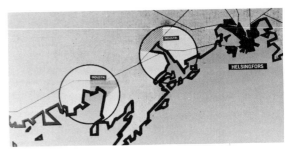

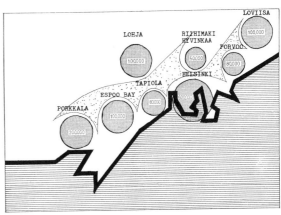

7.
Towns proposed in the
"Uusimaa 2010" plan. The
seven towns proposed in
1962 have become seven
regional groupings of
towns. (from "Uusimaa
2010," Helsinki, 1967)

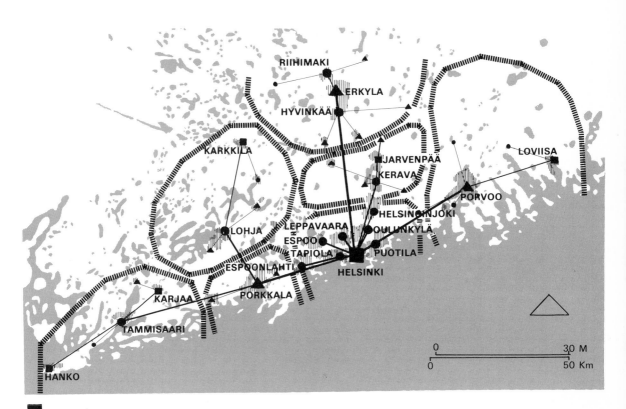

Primary and secondary centers

Tertiary centers, with direct access to Helsinki

A fourth-order center

A fifth-order center

A sixth-order center

A seventh-order center

Outline of a subregion. There are seven of these.

8.
Key for Plan of Tapiola

1. The fourteen-story central office tower (C)
2. The central shopping plaza (C)
3. Future theater and library (C)
4. Shops and offices ("Heikintori" department store) (C)
5. Lutheran Church (C)
6. Future hotel (C)
7. Swimming pool (C)
8. The Eastern (first) neighborhood center (E)
9. Four-story walk-up houses (E)
10. "Weak-link" houses and four-story walk-ups (E)
11. Walk-up houses (W)
12. Row houses (W)
13. School (N)
14. Row houses (E)
15. Prefab row houses (E)
16. Courtyard houses (N)
17. Row houses (E)
18. Walk-up houses (E)
19. Row houses (W)
20. Weak-link row houses (E)

To this common pattern Tapiola and Asuntosäätiö pose a clear alternative: building new towns
on a region-wide scale. Such a program can
avoid the problems inherent in trying to enlarge
old cities whose forms are not easily expanded.
Such a program evidences greater opportunity
for achieving broad social aims. Such a program
enables older towns to manage themselves better by relieving them of a type of growth that is
difficult to handle.

At this point in time, Tapiola and Asuntosäätiö's further plans constitute a striking alternative
to the normal patterns of urbanization witnessed
the world over. A proposal concerning this alternative was made in 1962, when von Hertzen
suggested that seven new towns be built in Finland's southernmost province, Uusimaa, the locale of Helsinki and of a large portion of Finland's urban growth. A precise study along these
lines was initiated in 1964 by Asuntosäätiö and
completed two years later. The study was entitled "Uusimaa 2010" (that being the target
year used in several other related studies). It
corroborated von Hertzen's 1962 proposal in
intent, while adding several important modifications and refinements. Most important, it supported the idea of a regional if not national outlook. Practically speaking, it meant a new towns
program.

New towns are by no means the sole answer
to the urbanization problems of Finland or any
other country. But, together with complementary
programs like the renewal of old towns, the new
towns idea has given convincing evidence of feasibility as well as the fulfillment of many social
objectives. The Tapiola experience also challenged the various policies and programs of the
Finnish government regarding what had been
accepted as their future pattern of urbanization.
Not only has it challenged them, it has caused
serious reconsideration and, it now seems evident, an alteration of the course of Finnish urbanization. A pattern that once seemed inevitable—overgrowth of existing urban centers—can
now be avoided and a substitute pattern undertaken: new towns on a regional scale.

While Tapiola presents its evidence in behalf of
nationwide new towns programs, that is not its
only relevance. Much of the daily know-how
learned in creating Tapiola Garden City as a
place to live is of considerable value. Again, new
towns alone are not the entire answer, nor are
garden cities the only possible form of new
towns. All concepts of urbanization, however,
can gain by an objective comparison with the
achievements of Tapiola. For urbanism every-
where Tapiola is a textbook.

Tapiola in Context

Historically, the idea of building new towns traces back to ancient times, and the reasons for building them are as numerous as the many societies in history. As numerous, too, have been the means at the disposal of various societies for building new towns—economic, technical, and institutional. Students of the subject have long been exploring these means and their consequent results. Their findings constitute a major body of knowledge in the field of urbanism in its many branches—politics, demography, geography, physical character, economics, social interaction, administration, law, commerce, industry, communications, and so forth. The intensity of investigation has grown rapidly, commensurate with a mounting awareness of the severity of urban problems. Often, the investigations have revealed reasons that have prevented or even discouraged the creation of a new town in circumstances that otherwise seemed opportune. That knowledge can be as valuable as the technical know-how needed for creating a new town.

Of course the more relevant information on new towns is derived from those created in recent decades, while a broader view of relevant new towns scans the last 150 to 200 years, the era of industrial technology. Because the experience of industrialization in countries that have known it has common ground (scientific technology, capital accumulation, opportunities for competitive investment, investment strategy, specialization of labor forces, political determination), the experience and consequent knowledge are of mutual interest. This holds for different places

and different times, different sites as well as different stages of development.

In a broad sense, then, an official in a developing African nation is a student of an earlier American or a later Russian experience in urbanization. So, too, may be a UN expert in South America or Cambodia. Not always are they aware that they are repeating the experience of other places and times. With luck and work they may learn through trial and error what works and what does not. If, however, they have available some measure of past experience, digested and made relevant to their circumstances, the hazards of trial and error are reduced and the chances for successful action are heightened.

The obvious point is that there is a body of experience and some documented information on new towns. It is not complete, but it is of some substance. It is not entirely digested or entirely formulated for ready usage because local differences preclude that. Thus, while the conditions that give birth to new towns may have common bases in different parts of the world, and while the composition of urban societies may also share common qualities, other differences exert their influence.

The experience of one country's efforts can be useful to another through careful selection. One must first determine the conditions for building new towns on native soil. Then one must understand the conditions of other places, to see where comparisons are possible, to see which distant experiences are relevant to local circumstances. Some plants thrive in a variety of soils; some develop adaptive mutations; all need a degree of selection.

Selection is no small task. One listing in 1963 named 300 new towns either built or in a serious stage of planning.* Further reference was made to a thousand or more that were elements of nationwide programs. All examples are of this century, most since World War II. They are located in every corner of the globe, in every climate, in societies in every stage of development. In short, new towns can be built for a number of reasons and under all sorts of economic, social, and financial circumstances.

The reason for building new towns in industrialized nations today is clear: by diverting urban growth from large existing urban settlements, the pressures of managing that growth are, first of all, relieved. They are relieved where relief is of considerable help. The proposition is that a better direction for urbanization lies in creating new towns wherein urban growth then becomes an opportunity rather than an added problem. Without adequate and effective policy and control, urban growth around a large urban center is haphazard. Even with policy and control, experience shows that the opportunities of realizing high levels of successful community building are still limited. If policies and programs are adopted to foster the creation of new towns in appropriate situations, unconstrained by a limiting existing urban fabric or a limiting development process, greater opportunities for achieving humane social objectives are afforded. It is an axiom of intelligent action that one start by choosing a course presenting the fewest hindrances. Of course new towns are often con-

* Sir Frederic Osborn and Arnold Whittick, *The New Towns: The Answer to Megalopolis* (New York: McGraw-Hill Book Company, 1963), pp. 141–148.

strued as being instruments of rural development, as in the case where a developing area needs an industrial center for processing or shipment. Such new towns are found in areas being developed for some national resource, such as metals mining and processing. But these are in a special category and of a somewhat different nature than the new towns currently held as an alternative to today's metropolitan urbanization.

The chief obstacle to new towns is that the nature of urban growth in industrialized societies does not favor the creation of new towns as much as it does the enlargement of existing cities. There are many reasons for this. Existing towns are where the people are. If they are in distress, they will insist on attention to their problems in their own habitats. So the programs of relief first of all go to where the wounded cry loudest. But there are deeper reasons for agglomerative urban growth. Existing cities are incubators for new enterprises. They possess numerous channels of supply and outlet, a choice of workers, a choice of premises. If one enterprise fails, other opportunities are near at hand. For the same reason, existing cities have wider job markets for workers. They also have associations and facilities developed over time, intricate, varied, and configured. Existing cities possess attractions not easily mustered in a newly made town. The very complexity and variety of an existing city attract new urban particles like a magnet. Incremental additions to existing urban tissue are more easily grafted than the wholesale creation of new and full-blown urban bodies. Even the familiar shortcomings and genuine discomforts of today's big city are far outweighed by the few alternative possibilities available else-

where to the average person. Willing or unwilling, he has little choice but to tolerate his urban lot. So it is that any endeavor to create new towns as independent or even partially independent entities works against a strong tide of trend. Such endeavors require great persuasion and effort, sustained over long periods of time.

Not the least of the obstacles to new towns is that a new towns effort requires a considerable national commitment over a long period of time and involves allocation of many resources. Few countries have been able or willing to make this commitment, even those aware of it. Fewer countries, still, are aware of the possibility that this kind of commitment need not conflict with other national priorities. In fact it can complement them. But even in those places where long-range commitments are entertained, short-range economic and social fluctuations can be upsetting. The commitment must be strong, and so must patience and a willingness to learn from experience.

Because the everyday conditions of industrial societies do not favor the new town, introducing a new towns effort is a confrontation with a vested status quo, generally a fractionalized status quo. It is not so much like harnessing a powerful stream as it is like joining a number of separate streams, combining the forces of the individual streams, all at once and in special combinations, in order to lend them a unified force that they would otherwise not possess. It is a matter of gathering random forces and mobilizing them to new purpose. In industrialized nations today these forces or streams are numerous. Few countries are similar in the degree to which they have conjoined the separate

streams. How does one identify the streams? What, in fact, are they?

They are financial institutions, for one thing. They are also marketing mechanisms. They are available investment funds. They are public utility construction programs; public services like health care and education; insurance rates; patterns of land ownership and practices in land development; land-use controls and land-use laws. They are private property rights and public powers of expropriation; building technology and building practices; consumer preferences and the climate for entertaining innovation. The very variety and complexity of the picture suggest that because the streams are so many the possible combinations should also be numerous and the options wide. One might think that a society possessing so many components could produce all sorts of community forms at command, but that is not always true.

Each of these streams is narrow, runs in a deep channel, and is neither easily relocated nor easily conjoined. Community building is an effort pursued by amalgamating numerous independent interests, public and private. Few can be ignored or easily circumvented. Thus, each of the separate interests, each of the requirements, each of the streams cumulatively narrows the range of possibility. Where the streams are most free, most developed, and most numerous—where the choices seem to be the greatest—the choices often are, ironically, the least. For instance, where the choice of specialized commodities and services (radios, cars, airlines, vacations, clothing, food) is wide, the choice in community types is scant. One speaks in such instances with a vocabulary limited in urban nomenclature,

of the city or suburb, uptown or downtown, the apartment or house. A fuller listing of choices requires only a modicum of terms and space. The problem is partly that a community cannot be produced like a single commodity or service. It is produced by many of them. To make them produce a real variety of community types, they must obviously be coordinated. Here, again, where there has been the greatest freedom for developing separate streams, separate commodities and services, coordination meets the greatest resistance. Yet the latent, potential choices remain numerous and varied. There are many possible types of houses, urban forms, landscapes, and environmental artifacts. There are many within a capability that we have hardly begun to tap. Books, magazines, and exhibits have been full of them over the last years. But the separate streams preclude their debuts on a popular scale.

The dilemma is dramatized by the disparity of what is possible and what is practiced. In the United States, for example, it is technically possible to build the entire mechanical core (heating, kitchen, bath) of a house as a unit and deliver it ready to work after connection. Modern airplanes have several washroom units, designed for maximum space efficiency. Where large-scale building coordination is practiced—as in Scandinavia (Finland included)—the ready-made bath is practical. But in the United States, one of the world's most advanced industrial nations, such units are illegal or impossible because of complex building restraints in most locales.

The streams resist. While autos, planes, elevator cabs, buses, and trains benefit from the greatest skills of industry, the same skills are barred from most of our housing. And, in the question of building whole communities, the streams show their greatest intractability. The streams will not easily be changed by propaganda, reason, public clamor, or even by an articulate professional appeal and prescription.

The severity of this problem in industrialized societies is one of degree and kind. In the United States, for example, the streams are numerous and their coordination minimal. The disparity between potential and product is large. In Sweden, indeed not a backward country, the streams are somewhat fewer, but their coordination is considerable and the disparity far less. The disparity relates inversely to the ability and willingness of a given country to grasp its streams of effort. In Canada one finds in existence many of the planning proposals long espoused in the United States: metropolitan government, more developed public transit, and public parking authorities, to name just three. It is a matter of degree of ability and willingness to grasp the streams. At issue is not the number of professional experts in a given country either. For experience shows that the capabilities of the experts are strongly related to what a society demands and is willing to support.

The experts have now begun to look at the processes of those places where the creation of the built environment is more successful. They have been investigating the areas where some of the streams have been successfully conjoined. They have looked at regional planning, metropolitan planning, new towns programs, industrialized buildings, and modernized administrative processes of several countries: England, Holland, Finland, Switzerland, Sweden, Germany, France, Israel, Russia, Poland. Urban bookshelves have begun to bulge with information. As information has accumulated, it has become quite clear that there are many stages or levels of stream gathering. How long a country has been trying, how dedicated it is to the task, how well prepared mentally for making alterations, how adept at inventing necessary instrumentalities—these factors determine its capability of grappling with its environmental problems. Such factors determine the likelihood of its success in building new towns as one environmental possibility.

Discerning the stages or levels of coordination is a crucial matter. In a country whose performance is low, it is easy to accuse the expert of wishful thinking when he looks to the processes of a more advanced country. Yet he may be discerning critical shortcomings in his own situation that might otherwise go unrevealed. And perceiving the critical shortcomings is a mandatory first step. The second step is to see what measures can be taken to improve processes.

All countries can learn from one another, including learning by rejecting bad habits. In the field of new towns, Sweden and Great Britain, both at relatively advanced stages, have much in common and many notes to compare. Countries in earlier stages of new-town development must look to other nations more like themselves. And those that have barely begun the process must look to countries that have just recently started, where the first fruits are still fresh, the early experiences still vivid.

The value of the experience of Tapiola, and its value to efforts elsewhere, is twofold. First, Tapiola and the proposed new towns of Finland present a complete picture in capsule form of the new towns thesis. In this example one can see the whole concept in outline. The new town is a corollary to solving the problems of large cities. This, in turn, requires a national program and adoption of a national policy. Second, the story of Tapiola itself, how it came about, how it was developed, what principles and practices underlay its creation—this in itself is a most worthwhile set of lessons. Thus, for countries needing a living and current example of a new towns program in action, here is a useful case study. It is pertinent to countries in a position to start building, as well as to those long in practice for whom some of Tapiola's design precepts and administrative procedures may be a refreshing surprise.

The thesis of this book is that Tapiola Garden City is full of lessons. It is especially significant that Tapiola was *not* a program of Finland's national government but was constructed by a company acting as a private but nonprofit business enterprise. Tapiola was built under stringent economic circumstances and tested in the competitive market. Since a major aim was to accommodate a real cross section of the population, the idea of new towns could seriously present itself to public and official attention and could seriously cause the latter to set a different course in national housing programs.

While the thesis of this book is to show the value of Tapiola's experience to other countries, its substance is simply to tell a story. This is a story of discerning a problem, selecting a plausible solution, and seeing it through. Tapiola starts at the beginning of the problem of urbanization, continues with a design solution and with administrative and managerial skill, and goes on to suggest the full realization of a national course for urbanization based on new towns.

2 Background

**New Towns and
Garden Cities in History**

There is very little new about "new towns."
They are the oldest form of planned community.
Hundreds, if not thousands, of towns bear
names like "villanuova," "villeneuve," "neu-
stadt," "newton," or "novgorod." And they are
new towns in the full sense, built as a whole
from the ground up. The ancient new towns
were, of course, colonial outposts, usually established to stabilize an outlying territory, as in the
Garonne River Valley of France in medieval
times or many pioneer areas of the United States
in the eighteenth and nineteenth centuries. Or
they might help funnel off excess population,
like Greek colonial towns throughout the Medi-
terranean or, later, Roman towns for settling old
soldiers in North Africa.

Today "new town" has a different meaning
and suggests an alternative to the vast, formless,
sprawling metropolis. It proposes instead succinct, manageable, livable urban units deployed
in urbanized regions. It is important to distinguish between the concept of independent small
towns and that of a series of interrelated towns
in an urbanized region. It is the latter concept of
new towns that is under discussion here, a form
offering a far more satisfactory arrangement than
today's typical and wasteful metropolitan sprawl.

In all aspects the new town idea evokes Aristotle's definition of a city: that it be large
enough to sustain itself in all its undertakings
but not so large that its inhabitants lose communication with each other. Much of the credit for
the new town concept of modern times is given
to eighteenth- and nineteenth-century utopian
philosophers. This credit is somewhat misplaced,
for while the utopians were writing of their
dreams, other men of action were building with
their hands. Leonardo da Vinci was one of these,
and he may be the true progenitor of the modern new towns hypothesis. He conceived and
saw partly built a regional canal system in northern Italy. That regional system for land development was, in his mind, a working foundation to
a network of satellite towns. He further conceived of a series of workers' towns and designed portable houses so that the workers could
live in town during the winter and in the country
in the summer. In the winter they would be employed in manufacturing, in the summer in agriculture. But a more direct ancestry to today's
new towns idea is traced to men of a more particular bent—early nineteenth-century industrialists and entrepreneurs. They built the direct
ancestors of today's new towns, which were of
two types: the workers' town and the satellite
residential community. Of the two, the workers'
town was the older form, for it can be traced
back even to the work camps of the pyramid
builders.

At the advent of industrialization, a handful of enlightened and innovating entrepreneurs built housing for their workers as adjuncts to the factories. Saltaire, Port Sunlight, and New Lanark are among the landmarks of England and Scotland. The Krupp factory towns are among Germany's accomplishments; the town of Chaux as well as the enlargement of Mulhouse are among France's. In the United States, Lowell, Massachusetts, and Pullman, Illinois, exemplify the worker-town concept. The motives of the industrialists were a blend of practicality and moral conviction. The industrialists realized that they would have to house their workers near their plants, or they would have no workers. Among the enlightened industrialists that realization was bolstered by the notion that healthy and happy workers were more productive.

The satellite residential town has less distant origins. It may have stemmed from the conception of the spa or country estate as happy appendages to urban life—and nineteenth-century urban life was quite open to alternatives. At the midpoint of the nineteenth century a model appeared outside of Paris: the small garden town of Le Vésinet, a commuter suburb built for the employees of a French railroad company. Shortly after, Riverside, Illinois, was begun outside Chicago. Designed by Frederick Law Olmsted, it was the first planned American dormitory town linked to its parent city by rail, as was Le Vésinet. From Riverside, one traces such accomplishments as Roland Park in Baltimore (1891), Forest Hills Gardens in Queens, New York (1911), and Mariemont in Cincinnati (1922). The outstanding design characteristics of both Le Vésinet and Riverside were their emphases on

greenery and spaciousness. The residential new town made its popular debut as a garden for living.

Although the satellite residential community and workers' town are the ancestors of current new town thinking, they were not the exclusive models. These were described in a book published in 1898 by Ebenezer Howard, an English inventor and social reformer. Titled *Tomorrow: a Peaceful Path to Real Reform*, Howard's book in a subsequent and better-known edition bore the title *Garden Cities of To-Morrow*.* It was based on Howard's observations on the theory and practice of nineteenth-century town building. His outlook was mainly social, but his persuasive power lay in outlining practical procedures for actually creating new towns—as garden cities. Their economic raison d'être would be their own enterprise, and their formation and construction would be based on workable programs of capital investment, joint land ownership, and sound developmental administration. Howard's enthusiasm for the feasibility of a widespread new towns effort was sparked by a visit to the American Midwest, where he saw prairie towns created almost overnight. The English new towns of Letchworth (1902) and Welwyn (1920) exemplified his theories in practice and constitute the historical landmarks of the new towns idea in garden city form.

*MIT Press Paperback, 1965.

A larger perspective of cities in their regional contexts was given by Howard's northern countryman, the Scottish biologist Patrick Geddes, who coined the term "connurbation" to describe the process of amorphous growth and decay experienced by industrial cities when urbanization proceeds unbridled.

In their broadest meaning, Howard's practical outline and Geddes' perspective have yet to be supplanted. Howard's ideas are often derided but more often misunderstood, for example, in the misinterpretation that he was "anti-city" or that he proposed a back-to-nature movement. Both Howard and Geddes proposed a better way to fashion cities as cities and, at the same time, to establish them as entities with nature. Their aim was to show society that they could have the best of both worlds simultaneously. In actual fact, too, Howard's and Geddes' philosophy have pervaded modern city and regional planning as or more extensively than any other body of thought.

The garden city form of new town stressed by Howard stemmed from his love of nature and the realization that man divorces himself from nature at considerable risk. It is worth reflecting on that every civilized culture has found a way to accommodate itself graciously to its natural surroundings. Howard's emphasis on a city in nature, as an intrinsic part of nature, proved to be one of the most appealing aspects of his concept.

In the United States, Howard's and Geddes' intellectual heirs were Lewis Mumford, Clarence Stein, Henry Wright, Catherine Bauer, and Benton MacKaye, to name a few. While the physical evidence of their work is sparse, it is convincing, more convincing for many than anything else achieved in America. Radburn, New Jersey, and the three "greenbelt" towns of the 1930s and TVA are among the better known results, along with a handful of towns built in World War I by the U.S. War Shipping Board and a few residential communities like Chatham Village in Pittsburgh or Baldwin Hills Village in Los Angeles. The social philosophy that found expression in TVA and the work of the National Resources Planning Board of the 1930s are vivid expressions of the attitudes of these pioneers.

Critics of the new towns thesis find the idea, in practice, to be wanting in one or more aspects. In a comprehensive introductory essay to the most recent edition of *Garden Cities of To-Morrow,* Lewis Mumford points out that a truly complete new town has never been built in America. Among the many that bear the name usually one aspect is stressed, like the garden city interpretation. The lack of regional planning is striking, and the full thesis remains an idea.

England has much more to show because of a national new towns program undertaken after World War II, the result of a long and strenuous national debate. Holland and the Scandinavian countries have a longer and more continuous experience. The town of Hilversum is one of Holland's older outstanding examples; the towns of Vällingby, Färsta, and now Skärsholmen are among Sweden's newer examples. France is in the midst of a vast program of new community

construction, around both its existing large cities and its older small ones.

If the recent new towns of importance today were to be listed, one would mention Cumbernauld, along with a few of the other English and Scottish new towns; Reston and Columbia near Washington, D.C.; Irvine in Southern California; Ciudad Guayana in Venezuela; perhaps Amsterdam South, although it is more of an appendage than a satellite; and Chandigarh and Brasilia. The list enlarges as classification boundaries expand. And although not all of these are garden cities, they all necessarily were conceived as towns in relationship to nature.

When Tapiola was started, not all of the more developed examples of today's new towns existed, and there were far fewer models to examine. In fact the "garden city" was nearly the predominant existing type of new town. One of the questions, then as now, concerning the habitability and suitability of garden cities was their urban quality, their urbanity. That question still requires debate, but certain of its aspects may now be more clear.

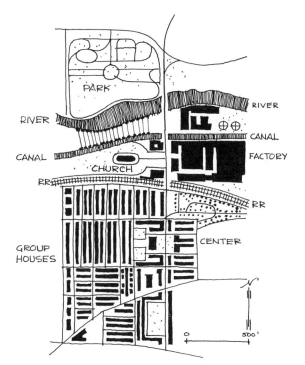

2.
The satellite garden city of
le Vésinet, about 10 miles
west of central Paris. It was
started in 1856 by
Alphonse Pallu as a private
enterprise. Its setting is an
eighteenth-century hunting
forest. The designers were
the Count of Choulet and
M. Olive. About 1200 acres
in size, its pre-World War II
population numbered about
12,000. Strict design and
land-use regulations were
imposed. Le Vésinet
anticipates many of the
features of the garden city
concept, but has the limited
function of a residential
satellite.

3.
Riverside, a suburban
community six miles west of
Chicago, designed by
Frederick Law Olmsted and
Calvert Vaux in 1869.
Astride the Des Plaines
River, and amply
interwoven with natural
greenery, it was connected
to Chicago by a commuter
rail line. Riverside embodied
the features that
characterized the later
American residential suburb.

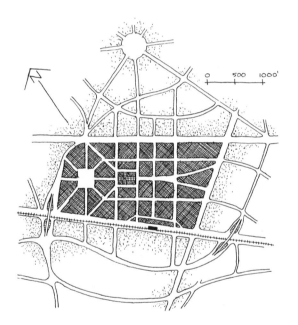

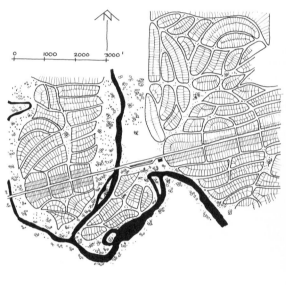

4.
Letchworth Garden City,
1903 (from *Garden Cities of
Tomorrow,* Ebenezer
Howard, MIT Press
Paperback, 1965).

5.
Welwyn Garden City, 1919
(from *Garden Cities of
Tomorrow,* Ebenezer
Howard, MIT Press
Paperback, 1965).

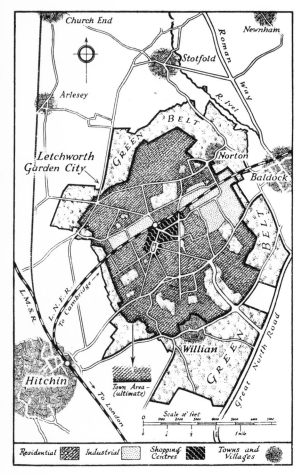

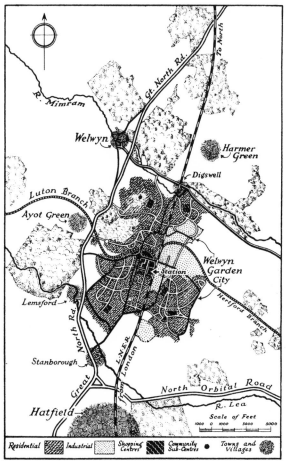

6.
Stockholm's new towns.
Central Stockholm is solid
black. Note the automobile
routes and the rapid-transit
lines.

7.
Plan of Cumbernauld.
Essentially it is a linear city,
with a spine of central
services. The perimeter is
housing plus two main
industrial zones.
8.
Air view of Cumbernauld,
Scotland, looking due
northwest.

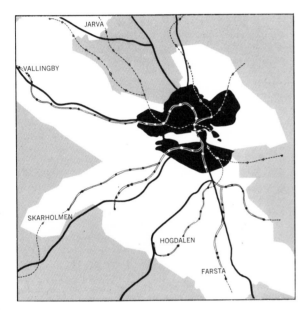

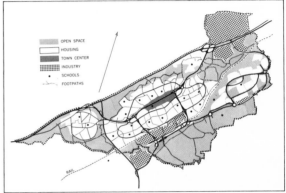

9.
Pullman, Illinois. Plan.
10.
Pullman, Illinois. View.
11.
View of Le Vésinet.
(Jean Houillon)
12.
A Street in Mariemont,
Ohio.

13.
Greenbelt, Maryland.
14.
Chatham Village. Plan.
15.
Chatham Village. View.
16.
Yorkship Village, Camden,
New Jersey, A World War I
worker's town.

17.
Radburn, New Jersey. An
inner pedestrian path.
18.
Cumbernauld, Scotland.
Town center.
19.
Radburn, New Jersey. A
vehicular cul-de-sac.
20.
Vällingby, Sweden. Row
housing.

21.
Farsta, Sweden. Row
housing.
22.
Farsta, Sweden. Town
center.
23.
Town center in Reston,
Virginia.

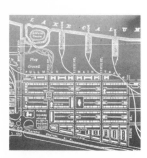

24.
Row housing in Reston,
Virginia.
25.
Concept for the town center
of Columbia, Maryland.
26, 27.
Environmental
misconceptions.

28–31.
Environmental
misconceptions.

32, 33.
Environmental
misconceptions
34.
The group of four single-
family houses in Itäranta.
35.
Miletus, Asia Minor. Plan.

36.
High-rise apartments in
Itäranta, designed by
Alvar Aalto.
37.
Patio house in the southern
neighborhood.
38.
Apartment houses in the
southern neighborhood.

Urbanization, Urbanity, and Urban Form

Certain issues regarding livability always arise in discussions of new towns. These questions revolve around the opportunities and activities found in contemporary metropolises as compared with the smaller new towns, One issue is that the garden city is antiurban, that the new town is an anomaly in urbanizing societies. On this point—the matter of urbanity or nonurbanity of the garden city—it might be useful to reconsider what in fact the term "urbanity" means.

It is possible that the current notion of urbanity has become confused with a city's sheer size and number of activities rather than the quality, diversity, and availability to all inhabitants of its opportunities and facilities. It is possible that bombardment of the senses has become confused with genuine communication, the fluid and constant exchange of ideas between people; that we have so many activities in our cities that they render each other partly inoperable; that the formlessness of the large city sets the stage for a uniformity which, in turn, is a seed bed for provincialism. Urbanity is not a matter of how much exists in gross but of how well things blend in daily experience. An urbane city furnishes many stimuli and the opportunity to digest them. Urbanity is the result of a long and conscious intention to render a city suitable to the free development of its people's senses and sensibilities. Urbanity is pursued over a long period of time, in fact constantly, if it is to be achieved and maintained. It is not a matter of the gross size of a city but of its intricate urban arrangement and consequent breadth of social opportunities, including contact with nature.

That the social and cultural characteristics associated with the term "urbanity" indicates the nurture of these traits in cities—at least in the cities of the past—does not mean that an urban setting is their exclusive habitat. Indeed the word "urbanity" may not have been well chosen, for the Chinese and Japanese landscape environment as well as the Western garden were no less the seats if not largely the incubators of humane social ideals prized by all civilizations. True, the city in history was the most frequent locale of exchange, if not confrontation, but it does not stand alone nor does it stand without imperfection as an influence on human social development.

A second issue is the idea that the new town concept is antithetical to the realities of contemporary urbanization. Here we ought to reconsider that phenomenon as a process. Urbanization is a process that operates in time. It requires an increasing number of people to live near one another. Urbanization characteristically accompanies industrial development. In the early stages of industrialization many laboring hands are needed to operate rudimentary machines. In later stages many of these hands are turned to administration and service, all of which make towns grow into cities and cities into metropoli.

Advancing industrialization accumulates wealth in terms of goods and services, which then elevates the process to higher levels. Affluence also requires, at least for a time, population proximity for distributing goods and services. That is the early stage of a metropolis. In even more advanced stages our means of transport and communication are improved, and we begin to spread out. The overall city—a metropolis—is a

large urban settlement, but at a density of settlement lower than the primitive industrial city. In other words many people live in the same region, serving one another, but each with more ample space, for all are more affluent. They can afford more space because they can afford better transportation while insisting on and consuming more goods and services. Thus we build a modern metropolis, a large gathering of people industriously producing and serving one another over a large landscape.

After a point, a major question confronts every metropolis: its size. How big can it be before certain disadvantages appear? Many answers have been offered, with little effect, for the world has numerous metropoli of many sizes, and in spite of their problems they continue to thrive. Inventive designers have often suggested startling technological or design solutions for the metropolis, solutions that would promise to make an even larger metropolis possible. They are seldom built, for the power of an idea, no matter how cleverly it utilizes technology, is but one factor shaping a metropolis. More powerful are the forces of social inclination, economics, and government; technology as a determinant is not about to replace them entirely. The question then turns to the livability of modern cities, and it is here that the modern metropolis shows its flaws, for despite many advantages the modern metropolis is not the most healthful place for people, socially or biologically. Given, then, the reality of forces available to shape our environment and build our cities, how can we do a better job? And how can we avoid the ills of the contemporary metropolis while we take advantage of the many real benefits it brings? Can the

solution be a matter of form?

The new town gives evidence of being a possible form. In this context the so-called new town is really a matter of how a metropolis is arranged in detail. In this sense, the new town idea proposes that the large metropolis be built as a series of succinct but interrelated and possibly interwoven pieces, each of much richer texture and activity than any portion of an ''unplanned'' metropolis. Most frequently, designs for a series of new towns are a pattern of built-up and open land. The built-up lands are the new towns, and they are separated from each other by open space. The open spaces, while essential, can be employed to link as well as demarcate the separate new towns. There are, of course, many variations. The new town, then, is really a social, functional, physical, and developmental entity, the basic component unit of an urbanized region. It is not so much an alternative to metropolis as it is a more workable form or design for the components of a metropolis. New towns comprising urbanized regions are a piece of contemporary metropolitan machinery for living.

A third issue stems from the early days of new town discussion, when proponents emphasized the idea that nearly all of a new town's wage earners would work in the town. This has proved difficult if not impossible to attain, and it has shaken the idea of the new town as an independent entity. Nevertheless, a fair degree of inhabitant employment is feasible and desirable. It may simply be a matter of having jobs nearer homes, so workers don't have to spend so much of their time traveling. If a metropolis were to be composed of a series of succinct new towns in

proximity and connected with good transport, the difficulty would be largely overcome. Of course, a good regional transport net would also be desirable anyway. The point is, however, that it has its limitations, too.

A key planning issue is the shape or form that cities might take, for different shapes have very real functional implications. It also happens that most of the theoretical work regarding shape remains theoretical. Little is actually tested in practice; most of the thinking is done on paper. On paper one draws models, graphically or verbally. Particular patterns come to represent to the theorist certain functional, social, or even aesthetic qualities. For example, the "octopus" form of metropolis implies high access to its center with large wedges of open space between its urbanized corridors. The "linear" form can be appended easily with lateral arms wherever needed. The "satellite" form adds orderly dependent units to its dominant central unit—and so on with the "constellation," the "ring," and the articulated or nonarticulated "sheet city."

These conceptual patterns are an indispensable aid to conceptual thinking. At the same time they can be inhibiting abstractions whose real implications are obscured. A conceptualization is merely an abstraction of reality. Essential details get little attention—but the little details happen to be where people spend their lives. A metropolis has to operate well as an overall entity and in its detail.

When Asuntosäätiö developed Tapiola, it was not aiming to realize an abstract planning conception on the ground. Its aim was "to create a modern urban environment for the modern city dweller." The garden city concept suited this end. To be free from bureaucratic hindrance and inflated land price meant building away from the edge of Helsinki. The garden city as a satellite suited these requirements, but it was largely excellence in detailed execution and management that underlay success. As to a choice of form, the garden city idea happened to be an extremely useful design concept for Asuntosäätiö. From every standpoint it suited its planning objectives—social, economic, developmental, managerial, and architectural. No other form offered as much as the garden city satellite during the time Tapiola was built.

It would be nonsense to conclude that Asuntosäätiö proposes bucolic decentralization or the dismantling of Helsinki. What is proposed is a plan for the further urbanization of Finland, which happens to make use of a tested planning idea and offers wide choice in residence, work, and recreation simultaneously. The forms employed by Asuntosäätiö suit these objectives. Very simply it is a case where form follows and abets function on a regional scale.

Justification aside, urban forms do not arrive full-blown out of the sky. Neither do architectural forms. Both have roots in history. Tapiola has antecedents in Finnish town building, as its buildings have antecedents in Finnish architecture. Both deserve acknowledgment.

39.
Urban forms:
octopus, linear, satellite,
constellation, ring, and
sheet. (after Kevin
Lynch, *Site Planning*
[The MIT Press, 1962]
p. 34)

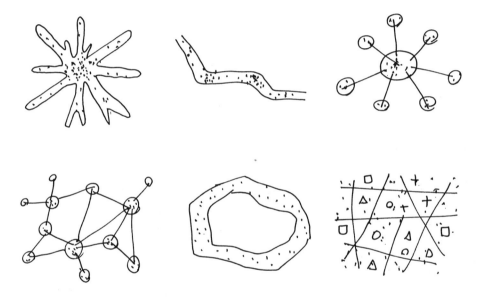

Architectural and Urban Design in Finland

In 1550, the Swedish King Gustavus I (Vasa) tried to establish a city on the south coast of Finland to trade with the Hanseatic town of Tallin, competing with Russia. He ordered the inhabitants of the towns of Rauma, Ulvila, Tammisaari, and Porvoo to move to a site at the mouth of the River Vantaa, which is near the present center of Helsinki. The site was on a shallow bay, unsuited for ships, and the venture failed. The settlers returned home.

Founding new towns for trade was not uncommon in Finland in the 1600s. Viborg is considered to be the first planned town, since it was enlarged and its fortifications rebuilt according to a plan. As a result a national assembly decreed in 1641 that all towns should be rebuilt according to the work in Viborg.

Another of the towns founded for trade was at Kruunuhaka—in 1640 on a rocky site. Growth was slow. The time had not arrived for making a large town. Then, in 1742, a retaliatory war with Russia was fought and lost. Finland ceded strategic border territory and so needed new defenses to protect its southern shores. The islands off Helsinki were the logical place for building land defenses. In 1748, Count Augustin Ehrensvärd began building the Suomenlinna fortifications on the offshore Helsinki islands. They were substantially completed by 1772, although supplementary work continued for another twenty years. Thus the seed of town planning was planted early in Finland, and so, too, the urban foundation that was to give Helsinki a dominant position. Finland formed part of the kingdom of Sweden from 1154 to 1809, when, as an autonomous grand duchy, it was united with Russia. Finland declared herself independent in 1917.

During the war of 1808–1809, the Russians occupied the Helsinki area. In 1808, an accidental fire burned the entire town. Lieutenant Anders Koche drew up a plan for reconstruction that proposed rebuilding along old lines in the old areas, with more generous layouts in the outskirts. The liberal-minded emperor of Russia, Alexander I, reestablished Finland's former laws, guaranteed autonomy, and in 1812 decided to move the capital away from Turku, which was located on Finland's southwest coast near Sweden. Henceforth Helsinki would be the capital.

In 1817, Johan Albert Ehrenström laid down instructions for a new town plan; to him can be credited one of the most handsome town designs of northern Europe. Ehrenström's imagination was fueled by visions of the classical Greek gridiron plan on a peninsula, with an open town square near the water—not unlike the plan of Miletus in Asia Minor. The plan laid down by Ehrenström enlarged the old market square so that it became Helsinki's main plaza. Rimmed with administrative buildings and dominated by a church, it still remains the administrative and symbolic heart of Helsinki. A broad esplanade separated the old town from the new and is still one of the main promenades of Helsinki.

40.
The Suomenlinna
fortification in Helsinki
Harbor. From 1748.

41.
Helsinki about 1810, prior
to the Ehrenström plan.

42a.
Plan of Helsinki by Johan
Albert Ehrenström. 1817.
A, Imperial Palace; B,
Lutheran Church; C, Greek
Orthodox Church; D, Public
Gardens; E, City Hall; F,
Commercial Warehouses; G,
Military Casern; H, Military
Cemetery; I, City Cemetery;
K, Basins for boats; L, New
Ropewalk (for ropemaking);
M, Royal Warehouses.
42b.
Plan of Helsinki, 1817,
showing the planned
portion in relation to its
larger peninsular setting.

43.
Miletus, Asia Minor.
Plan.

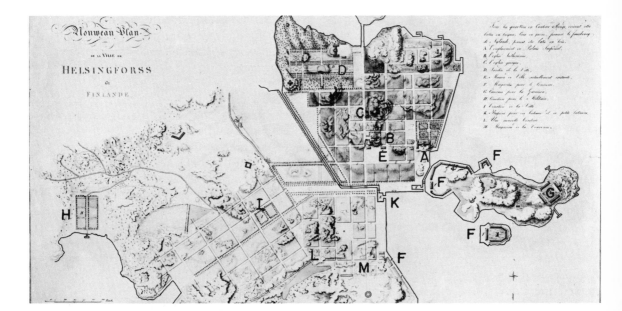

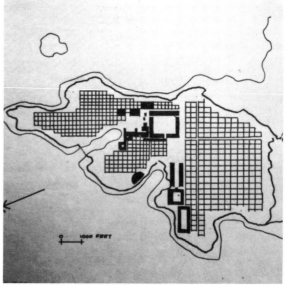

Architecturally Helsinki became a town of modest wooden houses and gardens, with three-story public buildings, the whole dominated by a classical dome on a plaza. For the translation of the plan into architecture Helsinki is indebted to the Finnish architect, Carl Ludwig Engel, a talented proponent of classical Hellenic design. Most of the old wooden buildings of Helsinki, which formed the overall setting for Engel's work, are now gone, but the impression of Engel's classical architecture still constitutes the main character of the older parts of Helsinki. By the time he died in 1840, Helsinki's population had risen to 18,000, more than a fourfold increase from the time when he started his work in 1816. It is worth noting that Engel held the position of controller of public works, in effect municipal architect, and that apprenticeship in this office was quite common for young Finnish architects.

In the early nineteenth century scarcely one Finn in twenty lived in a town. Even now a quarter of the population still consists of farmers. After Helsinki was founded, urbanization did increase. By 1856, it was necessary to establish a fire prevention code for building. Plans were formulated for the towns of Pori, Vaasa, Kemi, and Kuopio, among others, between 1838 and 1860.

The 1860s mark a decade of political liberality that, with the advent of railroads and industrialization, accelerated growth. In the 1870s building had increased to the point where four- to five-story houses were being erected. There was no land-use determination or zoning. Planning had degenerated to laying out rectilinear lots for building. Aesthetics was not among the considerations. Nevertheless, the building opportunities did open the door to innovation, and before the end of the century important design influences from abroad found their way into Finnish building.

Finnish architects had been working in a neoclassical style, with whose limited range they became uncomfortable. The Jugendstil movement of Europe offered a far freer palette of forms and appealed strongly to an urge to interpret nationalistic feelings in building. Traditional Finnish architectural details, shapes, and design motifs could enjoy a prominent position on the liberating Jugendstil palette. Here was opportunity to shape roof forms, to develop towers and turrets as focal points or vertical axes, to experiment with window patterns, and to embellish buildings with trees and shrubs as part of their architectural form.

The concomitant town-planning influences were being developed in Europe. Before the turn of the century the Viennese architect Camillo Sitte contributed his influential breakthrough in "artistic town planning" with his book *The Art of Designing Cities*. Sitte opened a new approach to planning that was functionally, socially, and aesthetically integral. And it offered restless architects rich opportunities for aesthetic inventiveness. Sitte's formulations were soon bolstered by the influence of the English garden city movement, through the dissemination of Ebenezer Howard's book, *Garden Cities of To-Morrow*. Helsinki's rapid growth furnished the opportunities to test the new design precepts.

44.
Senate Square, Helsinki.
The tall domed building is
the Cathedral of Helsinki,
designed by Carl Ludwig
Engel. (Finnish Air Force)

45.
The Cathedral of Tampere,
designed by Lars Sonck, an
example of ''National
Romantic style''—the
Scandinavian counterpart of
Jugendstil.

46.
The National Museum,
1910. This is a prime
example of the National
Romantic period. It was
designed by Gesellius,
Lindgren, and Saarinen
through a competition in
1901.

47.
A private home
designed by Onni Tarjanne,
1906.

In 1899, a competition for the Töölö district of Helsinki was held. The prizewinning entries were a proclamation and embodiment of the new direction, and a fresh page in Finnish architecture and planning was turned. In 1907, Eliel Saarinen designed the Helsinki railroad station, perhaps the principal statement of the freedom that the new architecture brought. In the same year the island "suburb" community of Kulosaari was successfully established, its layout in the theme of the 1899 competition. Saarinen himself soon went abroad to study new developments in European planning, as in Tallin and Budapest, which he reported back in Finland. In 1912, he won world attention for his submission of a design for Australia's capital at Canberra.

In 1915, he produced his plan for the Munkkiniemmi-Haaga area, which proved to be a decisive influence on the 1920s. The plan was presented in elaborate book form, with population maps, rendered plans and elevations, and photos of an incredibly detailed model of the entire area. The houses and streets had a Parisian air, but with front and rear gardens added. Definite differentiation in street types was indicated. A main through-traffic artery was sunk below grade. Saarinen had produced a text of modern town planning.

Saarinen's definitive statement of planning is his 1918 prizewinning entry for a general town plan for greater Helsinki, a year after Finland achieved her independence from Russia. This plan remains one of the best expressions of the concept of a satellite city, at the scale of streetcar transit, which is to say preautomobile. The plan proposed a series of satellite communities separated by open space but connected by a streetcar system. In this plan the Tapiola site was shown as one of the satellite communities. The area was then called "Hagalund," or "woodland meadow," the name it retained until "Tapiola" was substituted in the 1950s.

The influence of functionalist architecture in the 1920s was the last lubricant needed to free completely the imagination of Finnish architects. It freed them without substituting one doctrine for another. Between 1921 and 1924, a small garden suburb called Käpylä was built on the edge of Helsinki. The site concept followed Ebenezer Howard's suggestions for garden cities, but the buildings, simple wooden structures, recalled old Finnish building traditions. With all the accomplishments of Finnish architecture and site design since then, Käpylä remains a favorite. Visiting architects are invariably taken there by the Finnish hosts, usually after they have seen more spectacular recent work. It is as if Käpylä were a landmark for them, as if it proclaimed, "You see, we have long had a rich palette, but we are very conscientious about doing the most appropriate thing. We do not always have to demonstrate our virtuosity."

48.
The second-prize design for
the Töölö area of Helsinki,
by Lars Sonck, 1899. This
covers the same area as the
Nyström plan.

49.
The first-prize design for the
Töölö area of Helsinki, by
Norrmén and Gustaf
Nyström, 1899. This shows
the central area of their
plan. Water is at the lower
left and upper right.

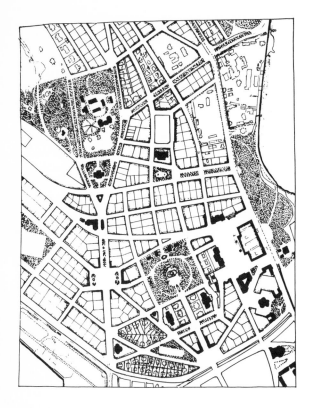

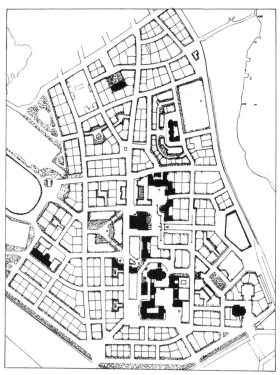

Finnish architects have always had a feel for town planning and for rural siting. In their city work they are assured urbanists, in their rural work sensitive naturalists. The years since their design freedom was won have been dotted with architectural landmarks. Alvar Aalto designed the Sunila pulp factory and workers' town from 1936 to 1939. Hilding Ekelund and Martti Väli-kangas designed the Olympic Village just before World War II. During the war Aalto worked on his experimental town designs. In the years following the war, town planning took a great upsurge. Otto-I. Meurman drew the initial plan for Tapiola in 1945 and 1946, when the site was still called Hagalund and six years before Asuntosäätiö was formed. His plans were drawn for a private client.

In 1946, Helsinki annexed land to increase its territory from about 115 to 625 square miles, nearly a sixfold increase. In 1949, a competition was held by the municipality of Helsinki for the central city. The outcome was recognition of a new level of requirements for the central area, including Töölö Bay, an inlet of the sea on the northern edge of the old city. New patterns of circulation were proposed, new land-use patterns were suggested, and an expanded concept of form for Helsinki came under discussion.

Alvar Aalto's name is one most frequently heard in connection with Finnish town planning, due to such works of his as the master plan for the Finnish Technical Institute at Oraniemi (alongside Tapiola's eastern edge) and his town plans for Imatra near the Russian border. Commissioned by the city of Helsinki, Aalto has given much thought to this area over the years. He envisions the capital as the lively and vital heart of the nation, the capital city grown into a metropolis. The old civic center created at the time of the czars and consisting of the market place–senate place complex should be kept as it is. The location of the parliament building on Töölö Bay determines the position of the new center. On the western shore of the Bay, as a continuation of a triangular piazza, the following monumental buildings will be situated: the congress hall, the concert hall, the opera, the art museum, and the municipal library. Three or four additional sites are reserved for future public buildings. They will be flanked on one side by the water and on the other by an existing park. Under the square there will be parking space for 4,000 automobiles. Together with an additional parking space for more than 6,000 cars, it will handle parking for the new center. This project has already begun. The present Helsinki plan envisions a central city population of well over 600,000, road and parking for vastly increased auto usage, a subway system, and the northward extension of the functional center of Helsinki. Growth would thus enlarge but not strangle the center.

Many other Finnish architects deserve recognition for their contributions to environmental design, but it is just as important to acknowledge the circumstances within which they worked. These circumstances spelled the difference between the realization or the neglect of their designs. Asuntosäätiö, for one, was an organization through which designs could be realized. While its work on Tapiola was progressing, the national government of Finland was formulating policy on housing and urbanization. That now stands as the larger context in which environmental design is practiced in Finland, and it must be presented here. At the same time, however, it should be remembered that the programs described were not available to Asuntosäätiö until well after Tapiola was started and had proved itself.

50a,b.
The railway station in
Helsinki, designed by Eliel
Saarinen. Designed 1904;
built 1906–1914.

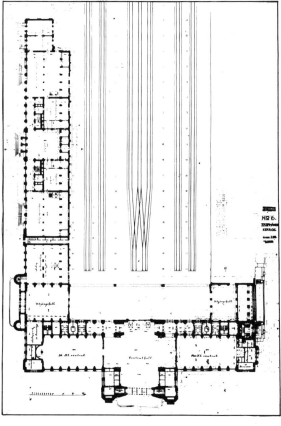

51.
Kulosaari garden suburb,
designed by Lars Sonck,
1907–1908.
52.
Eliel Saarinen's second-prize
entry for the capital of
Australia, Canberra, 1912.
(The first prize was won by
an American and
contemporary of Frank
Lloyd Wright, Walter Burley
Griffin.) Saarinen's design
brought him international
recognition.

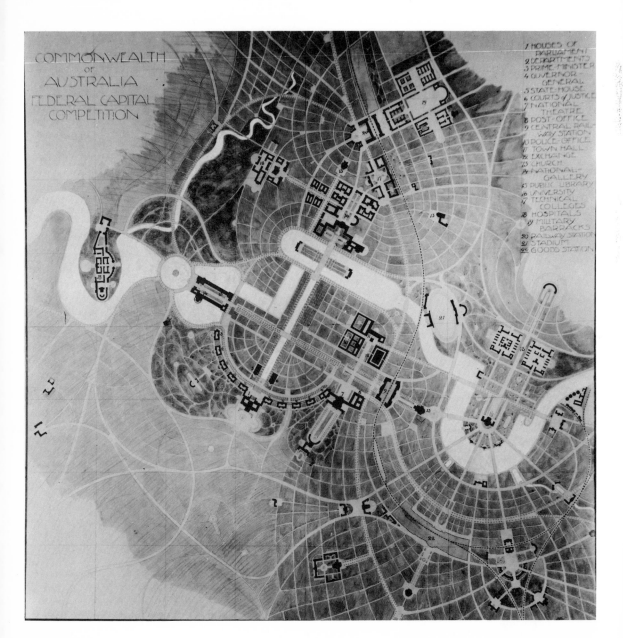

53.
Eliel Saarinen's plan for the
Munkkiniemmi-Haaga area
of Helsinki (i.e., its outlying
northwestern quadrant).
This was done in 1915.
The plan was preceded by a
probing analysis of the
entire city of Helsinki and
its future needs. (from
"Munkkiniemmi-Haaga,"
1915)

54.
A section of the model of
proposed "Munkkiniemmi-
Haaga."

55.
Eliel Saarinen's plan for
greater Helsinki, 1918. The
site of Tapiola is shown as
a developed area. It is
labeled "Björnvik
Hagalund" and lies on the
left edge of the plan, about
a third up.

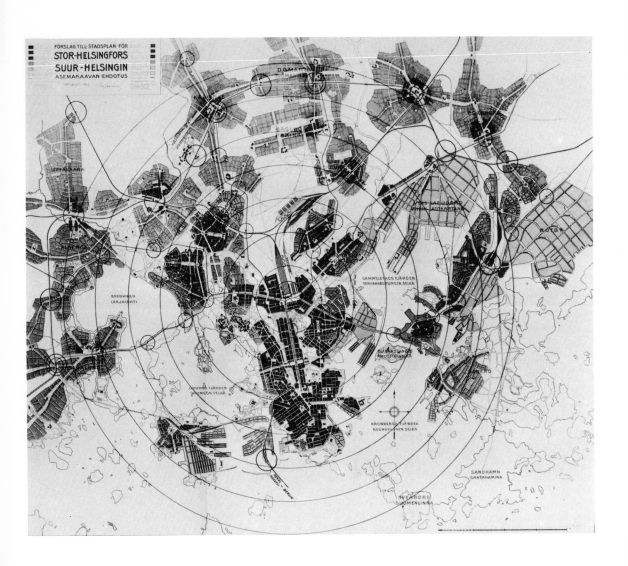

56.
Birger Brunila: Plan of
Käpylä Garden City, 1919.
The drawing is by Otto-I.
Meurman, who later made
the first plan of what was to
become Tapiola.

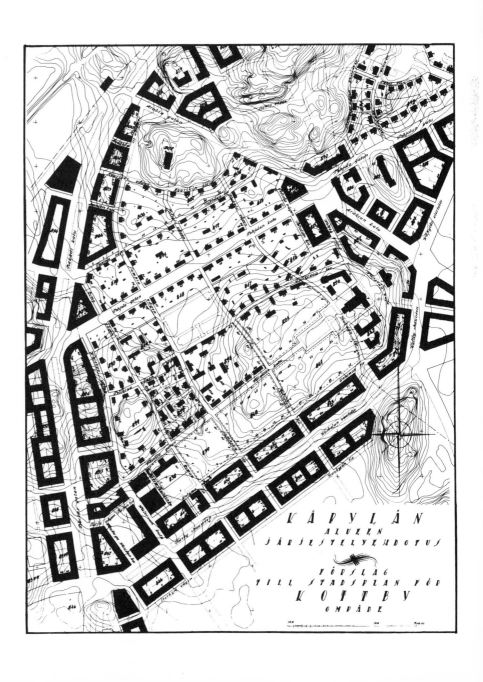

57a,b,c.
Buildings in Käpylä,
designed by Martti
Välinkangas, Birger Brunila,
and Akseli Toivonen,
1920–1925.

58a,b,c,d.
The Sunila cellulose factory,
with its housing areas,
designed by Alvar Aalto.
1936–1939.

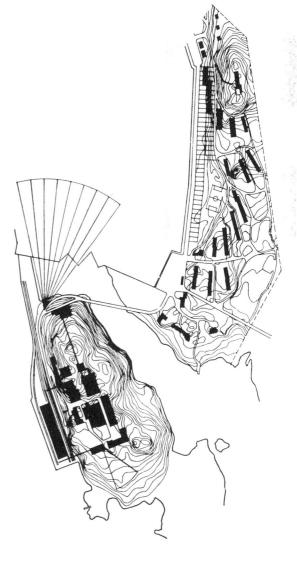

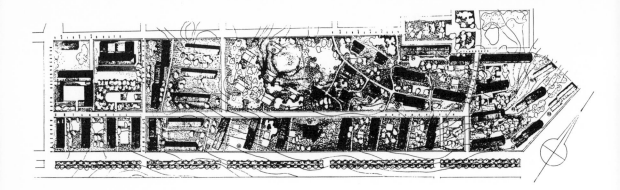

59a,b,c.
The Olympic Village in
Helsinki, designed by
Hilding Ekelund and Martti
Välinkangas, 1939–1940.

60a.
Site plan for the Finnish
Technical Institute at
Otaniemi, by Alvar Aalto,
1949. The site of Tapiola is
alongside, just to the west
(left).

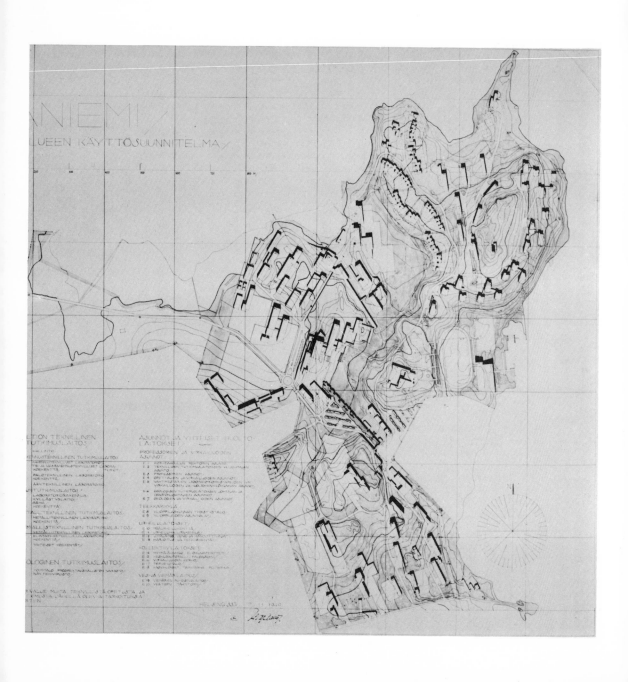

60b,c.
The center of the
technical university, at
Otaniemi, designed by
Alvar Aalto, 1962–1965.

60d,e.
The student union
building, "Dipoli," at
Otaniemi, designed
by Reima Pietilä and
Raili Paatelainen,
1964–1966.

61a,b.
Plan for central Helsinki.
This is one part of a more
extensive plan. The building
on the left is the National
Museum. To the right along
the shore of Töölö Bay are a
congress hall, concert hall,
opera, art museum, and
municipal library. The
fanlike terraces in the
foreground are parking
garages. The plan has been
in preparation since 1959,
under several architects,
including Alvar Aalto.

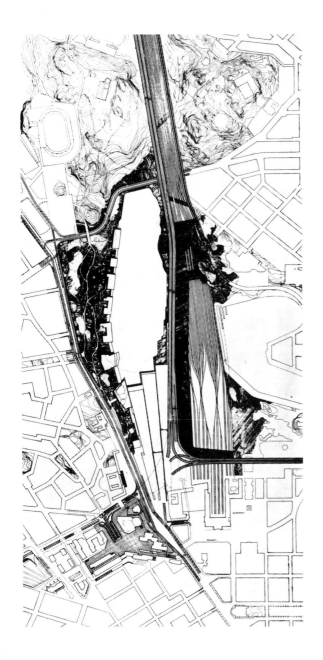

Finland's Housing and Planning Programs

Finland's housing programs were shaped by the circumstances of the last half century, as have been the housing programs of almost all Western countries. World War I had brought all Finnish building to a halt, but the late 1920s saw a government subsidy program for urban areas and a house-building boom—followed by the depression. In the mid-thirties many small homes were built, partly spurred by the 1936 Resettlement Act, which offered low-interest loans to manual workers. World War II, really two wars for the Finns, saw an interval of development in prefabrication methods but, more serious, the loss of an eighth of the entire housing stock. In addition, Finland lost 12 percent of its land to Russia. This land had accounted for 10 percent of the country's productivity. Further, Finland was saddled by a $570 million war reparations debt to Russia, to be paid over an eight-year interval. (Payment was completed in 1952.)

Nevertheless, after World War II building activity was intense, despite shortages of capital, labor, and material. The government subsidized housing for those who had lost their homes in the war, at an interest rate of 3 percent. Three-fourths of the houses were built in rural areas, which caused rural sprawl and severe strains on urban housing. In 1948, the Housing Tax Relief Act was passed to stimulate urban housing, and in 1949 ARAVA, the State Housing Board, was created. In the first half of the 1950s, house production was still concentrated in the rural areas, but this picture changed swiftly in the latter years of the decade because of the new emphasis. By the mid-sixties, three-fourths of the new housing was urban. The extent of housing activity in Finland is illustrated by the fact that a quarter of the country's investments were for housing in the 1950s.

The main problems in production were a shortage of credit and the backwardness of home loan activities. This led to a situation where the builders and the people in need of housing developed a method of financing. Previously, short-term credit exigencies had been the basis of housing credit policies. Thus, through the last half century or more, one can trace the development of home loans by savings banks, cooperative banks, insurance companies, commercial banks, and the State Postal Savings Bank. In other words, house financing gradually became more institutionalized.

ARAVA was the single most important factor in house production since World War II. Its objective was housing in urban areas. It gave loans at 1 percent interest over 33 to 45 years. Revisions in its program were made in 1953 and again in 1959. Between 1949 and 1966, over 160,000 dwellings were built, of which about two-thirds are rental or owner-occupied apartments. Half of Finland's present housing stock was built since World War II.

Other incentive means were also employed, such as tax exemptions that attracted private capital to house production. The exemptions covered the houses, the lots, capital investments, income, and building materials. Housing allowances are given by the government to low-income families with children in rented dwellings. Local communities and charitable institutions take care of the elderly, for which purpose the National Pensions Institute lends money at 3

percent. One popular route to home ownership
is the "save for a home" program. Aspiring
homeowners voluntarily build up their savings in
banks with the objective of accruing a deposit,
quite substantial in Finland. Municipalities are
exempted from the land transfer tax (from 3 to
12 percent) which induces municipal ownership.
Other policies also put land into municipal ownership and encourage development.

As a result of reexamining the housing situation, the National Housing Board was established in March 1966, as successor to the State
Housing Board. Not all of the Act is in effect at
this writing, but it has the following purposes:
1. To achieve steady growth for housing.
2. To prepare a national program for housing.
3. To regulate community housing programs.
4. To give loans and guarantees, subsidize interest, award research grants, and give housing allowances.
5. To make proposals for annual housing appro-
priations.
To centralize administration, the Housing Board
is placed under the Ministry of Internal Affairs.

Building practices in rural areas are quite different from those in urban areas. In rural areas
builders and buyers are largely private individuals. In urban areas, on the other hand, "housing companies" are founded, organizations established to build group dwellings. In some
cases the towns are major shareholders in these
"housing companies," whose main purpose is
often to accommodate those whom the normal
market excludes by building for them directly.

The housing companies range from those entirely privately financed to those financed
through government programs or subsidy.
Shareholders in subsidized housing companies
own shares and are entitled to permanent ownership of an apartment or dwelling. One buys a
dwelling by buying shares. The sale price of
shares in subsidized housing is, of course, con-
trolled; in nonsubsidized housing it is not. There
are also housing cooperatives, as contrasted with
housing companies. In the "coops" one is a tenant, not an owner, and rents the dwelling. In
coops the shareholder invests up to 10 percent;
in government-subsidized ownership housing
companies, up to 30 percent; in private companies there are no limitations.

Housing companies are created by various combinations of future occupants, by contractors, by
municipalities, and by nonprofit housing societies. Altogether, they build about half of Finland's housing—while taking care not to circum-
scribe the means of housing availability, which
would prevent flexibility in the housing market.

Asuntosäätiö is an example of a nonprofit housing society, itself created by six other nonprofit
organizations, put in operation in 1952. HAKA
is another nonprofit housing society, set up by
43 nonprofit organizations. SATA is still another,
backed by 24 companies, including industry,
building materials manufacturers, contractors,
and townships. Asuntosäätiö differs largely from
HAKA or SATO in that its aim, from its incep-
tion, was to build whole communities with complete facilities, not just housing.

Building construction in the Finnish countryside is a handicraft operation on a small scale. In the city commercial contracting companies of medium size are the rule. Many are joint-stock companies. As elsewhere, there are also specialized subcontractors. Half the country's building workers are employed in dwelling construction, and policies are directed toward their employment in the slack winter months. Seasonal unemployment still presents problems, however.

Overall, about half the Finns own their homes, and home ownership is rapidly rising. In 1950, less than a third of the urbanites owned their homes; now over 40 percent do. Rural people are more often homeowners. Courtyard and row houses are a good compromise for the decreasing number of detached houses built. Housing standards, as measured in amenity, size, and facilities, are rising, but overcrowding is still a problem.

Changes in population composition by age, occupation, and family size are exerting a marked influence on future house production planning, compounded by the trend to urbanization. Sixty percent of the population is now urban, and this ratio will increase to 75 percent in 1980. Over 50,000 dwellings a year will have to be built in the 1970s to meet these changes and growth—this in a country of about 4½ million people. But this is a goal that is not yet achieved.

Finnish building regulations are embodied in the Planning and Building Law (Parliamentary) and Building Act (Government Administration) enacted in 1959. The Building Law concerns land subdivision regulations and makes town planning mandatory. It also governs building bylaws or codes, regional and town plans, land ceding and appropriation, compensation, public utilities, and town planning in rural communities. The Building Act is more concerned with procedure and responsibility. To a very large extent authority is placed in local hands. An interesting exception is that the construction of large subsidized projects are keyed to fluctuations in employment by the state agencies responsible for labor and public works. This helps counteract employment slumps.

Finnish planning, also under the Building Law, is supervised by the Ministry of Provinical Governments and Internal Affairs. Finland's self-governing townships are responsible for making and implementing their own plans. The townships supervise their local building projects, but the Ministry of Internal Affairs supervises their actions and their performance. Expenses for planning, implementation, inspection, and supervision are shared by both. The landholder also pays a part of these expenses.

Planning is done at several levels, depending on jurisdiction, geography, and need.
1. Town Plans are made for dense population areas and are quite detailed.
2. Master Plans are outline schemes for the future for the development of cities, towns, and rural communities.

3. Regional Plans have been made through both statutory and voluntary compacts and quite obviously are ambitious in scale and outlook. The compacts are called "regional planning associations." Southern and southwestern Finland are already covered by obligatory regional plans, and the regional planning area will in the near future comprise the whole country.

There are several regional planning efforts under way, but none with an officially adopted plan as yet. Such planning, however, traces back to 1940; nationwide planning may be traced back to 1951. The Ministry of the Interior has the foremost responsibility for planning at all levels, and it sets policy. The National Planning Office, created in 1956, recommends and advises on urban development and production. The most recent town planning competition of note was for the town of Espoo, just north of Espoo Bay and northwest of Tapiola. The design was made by a team of Polish architects and planners. A number of areas in Tapiola were designed through competitions of several kinds, and these will be described later.

Organized building research is relatively new in Finland and is mainly concerned with materials and methods. The most important center is the State Institute for Technological Research in Otaniemi. Standardization was initiated by the problems of the postwar housing shortage, but by no means is this operation as extensive as it should be. The Association of Finnish Architects (SAFA) established a Standards Institute, which periodically issues data sheets to architects and builders. Civil engineers, materials manufacturers, and builders also conduct research and are constantly improving practices.

Traditional construction technology predominated until 1956, at which time larger scale on-site building operations took over. In the 1960s extensive prefabrication methods came into play. Many components are now produced in plants off-site. Computers are increasingly employed for building coordination. By 1966, over half of the multifamily government-subsidized housing was prefabricated, and over a third of the detached houses were standard models. Finland exports prefab wooden houses.

ARAVA was created to grant inexpensive housing loans, a function fulfilled successfully. Its replacement, the National Housing Board, attempts to go further, dealing with national housing policy as a whole. As such, it will engage in research and planning.

Certain other factors are relevant. Because winter is long in the northern European countries, housing requirements are much greater there than in some parts of central Europe. Heating equipment and insulation in dwellings must guarantee a temperature of 68°F (20°C) during the coldest weather without unduly high heating costs. The northern climate makes the dwelling the center of family and social life. Thus the requirements as to the size of the dwelling are higher than they are in countries where everyday life and leisure-time occupations are less home-centered.

Despite legal requirements concerning minimum floor areas, Finland's housing stock consists of dwellings that are, on the average, smaller than in western European countries. According to the 1960 census average dwelling area was only 550 square feet (51 square meters) and the area per dweller about 150 square feet (14 square meters). The average area of the dwellings produced in the 1960s has been about 680 square feet (63 square meters). The average area per inhabitant has also increased in the 1960s, although quantitative housing objectives have not been fully achieved. In 1968, the average was 755 square feet (70 square meters).

The main reason for the small size of the dwellings is high housing costs. For instance, in new government-subsidized apartment houses, monthly rents may be as high as $0.13 per square foot (6 marks per square meter), which means a rent of $100.00 (420 marks) in a dwelling of 750 square feet (70 square meters). This applies to the Helsinki region. The average rent in the country is lower. In houses that have not been subsidized by the government, the average level of rents is greater by $9.50 (40 marks) for similar dwellings. As compared with the monthly wages of Helsinki industrial workers, this means well over 25 percent of income. The housing costs of families with several children are lowered to some extent by means of a housing allowance. Yet the high housing costs are one reason that the mother of every second family holds a job.

The most influential factor in high housing costs is the shortage of investment capital. The interest rate of loans is high (about 8 percent), and there are not many sources of long-term mortgage credit. The amortization period of bank loans for government-subsidized houses is 22 years, but the loan period for all other houses is usually 5 to 15 years.

Building techniques necessary in cold climates and the small size of the dwellings further increase building costs. On the other hand, the building costs of multistory houses include the costs of heating equipment, kitchen (stove and refrigerator included), and bathrooms. In the biggest cities the high cost of land has a marked influence on housing costs.

More than 20,600 families with children now receive the special housing allowance. The allowance reduces the housing costs of low-income families with several children to a level not exceeding 25 percent of the family's total income. The percentage of income for rent was 36 to 37 percent for families without the allowance, 20 to 21 percent with. The housing allowance paid 20 to 70 percent of the rent. (It should be remembered that none of this existed when Tapiola was begun.)

Government loans for the construction of owner-occupied dwellings are thus divided into two groups: basic loans and additional loans. The maximum amount of a basic loan is 30 percent of the building cost, and the maximum loan period is 25 years. Basic loans are granted to housing companies (developers) for the construction of entire houses and, as personal loans, for the construction of a one-family house. They can also be used to purchase shares entitling

ownership of a unit in a multiple dwelling that has not received a government loan. All the houses in which one or more dwellings have been granted a basic loan must be approved by the National Housing Board for design and construction and cost.

The motivation behind the additional loan is basically social, but it has, in addition, a strong influence on production. The additional loan enables many families to acquire a dwelling of their own. Otherwise their only choice would be a rented dwelling. When a dwelling is subsidized with a possible additional 30 percent loan, the amount financed by the family may be as low as 10 to 30 percent of the total cost. Thus, additional loans make it possible to attract even small savings to housing production.

Government-subsidized apartment houses in which the dwellings are rented are built for families that cannot acquire dwellings of their own, even with the help of low-interest government loans. For such houses, the government loan amounts to 60 percent of the cost. The interest is 1 percent for the first five years and 3 percent thereafter. The loan period is 45 years.

Many improvements are needed in the entire system. The need of a national physical plan has been much discussed. At the lower levels of planning there is an urgent need for a decision on optimal physical land use and development. It is of the utmost importance to create a few centers capable of effective development at the regional level. Housing, land-use, and transportation policies in urbanized areas must also be coordinated.

Finland has made a good start in regional planning. A "structural plan" will be completed for all the fourteen regional planning districts, as a result of a planning directive from the Ministry of Internal Affairs. The structural plan includes the systematization of different types of centers as well as major communications elements. Existing legislation makes regional planning possible in the whole country; it will also make planning more efficient. An especially urgent task is the establishment of natural areas that are to be preserved untouched in each region. Decisions must also be made with regard to the reservation of land for recreation and tourism near urbanized areas.

At the local level there are, at present, strong tendencies to combine all local planning under one local authority and to establish better links between local public planning authorities and private developers. Many urban communities are establishing building registers. These registers will serve as local data banks in cooperation with the development of national demographic, building, and other registers. This will make it possible to keep an eye on development in the field and to use computers for planning. The new law makes master plans compulsory in all urban municipalities and in larger rural communities too. Since long-term functional and economic plans are, moreover, becoming much more common, there are fewer obstacles to effective physical planning at the local level.

The establishment of an autonomous regional administrative level is necessary to coordinate the duties of national and local authorities, thus making planning efficient. In regional planning the present tendency is toward larger planning units corresponding to administrative and economic districts. These would act, at the same time, as decision-making and implementation bodies.

Up to now planning has been mainly concerned with the enlargement of existing areas and with the development of new housing areas around old towns. It has not been possible to develop new towns as a general policy because the expropriation laws are not sufficient for these purposes. At the time that Tapiola was started, raw land was acquired through voluntary purchase.

Problems of urban renewal are few because there are no slums. The postwar resettlement policy—over 10 percent of the population had to resettle in an area of under 8,000 square miles (20,000 square kilometers)—resulted in a cumbersome division of land that has had a retarding influence on planning. Rational planning has also been handicapped by the freedom of the landowners to subdivide their lands and the lack of any controls in such subdivision.

At a national level the lack of efficient national planning and the appropriate policy concerning developing areas are severe problems. Most of the country is described as a ''developing area.'' The government has yet to favor the creation of functionally efficient urban centers. There is insufficient coordination between various special branches of government at the national and regional levels. Cooperation between planning, road, transportation, waterway, cultural, social security, trade, and other authorities is not sufficiently flexible. Cooperation between the communities is, for the time being, mainly voluntary. Lack of flexibility in administration has been one of the main handicaps in the coordination of planning and economic objectives.

Lest these facts suggest that Tapiola had the advantages of the programs described earlier, let the reader be reminded again that none of this existed in the early 1950s when Tapiola was started. It all happened in a country with extremely limited resources.

62a,b.
ARAVA-financed housing in
Tapiola: ''Mäntyviita''
apartment house, designed
by Viljo Revell, 1954. This
house is made of prefabricated wooden elements.

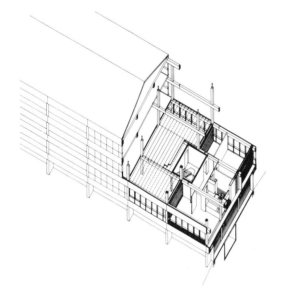

63a,b.
An ARAVA-financed
apartment house in Tapiola:
"Kaskenkaatajantie,"
designed by Viljo Revell,
1958. (Revell was also the
designer of the Toronto City
Hall, which he did in a
competition.) (scale 1:220)

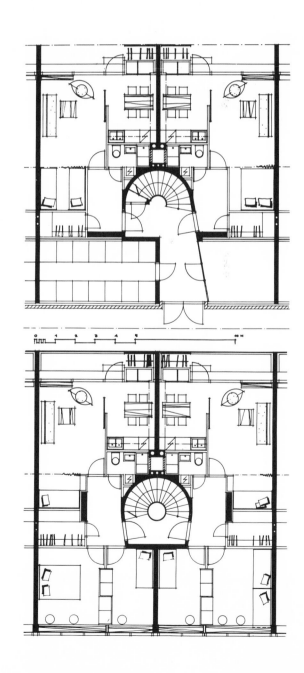

64a.
ARAVA housing in Tapiola.
Row houses in the
"Kontiontie" area, designed
by Kaija and Heikki Siren,
1955.

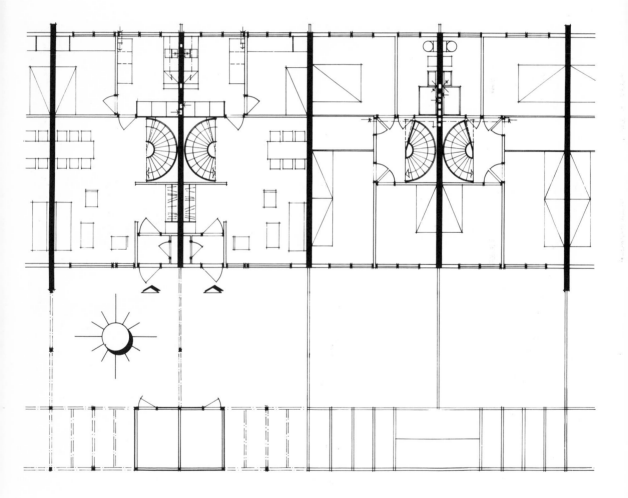

65a.
ARAVA-financed housing in
Tapiola: the ''Kaskenpaja''
and ''Allakka'' apartment
houses, designed by Aulis
Blomstedt, 1965.

APPARTEMENT HOUSES: "KASKENPAJA" AND "ALLAKKA" / TAPIOLA / FINLAND / SCALE 1/100 / TYPICAL PLAN / AULIS BLOMSTEDT ARCHITECT

66a.
Plan for Espoo Center,
1967. This was the result
of a competition. It was
won by a team of Polish
architects, J. Chmielewski,
J. Kazubinski, and K. Kuras.
The plan closely resembles
a recent proposal for the
town of Toulouse, France.

66b.
The town center of Espoo,
from the competition entry.
The concept is to separate
pedestrian and vehicular
traffic, pedestrian traffic
being organized on branch
system.

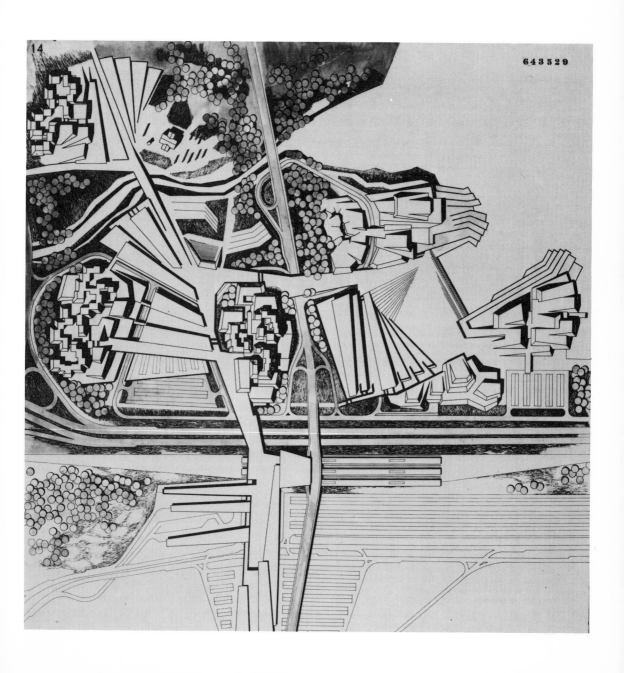

Facts and Figures

Finland is 335 miles wide and 720 miles long with 685 miles of coastline. The total size of the country is 130,000 square miles (Great Britain is 94,220, Western Germany, 95,760, and Italy, 116,220 square miles). Finland has one of the lowest population densities of all European countries—4.7 million inhabitants (Sweden was 7.9; Denmark, 4.8; Norway, 3.8 million). Roughly 36 inhabitants per square mile occupy a country whose total size is half that of Texas. Forests occupy 71 percent of the land, 16 percent is wasteland, and 13 percent is cultivated. The best farmland as well as the majority of the population is in the south. Nearly a tenth of the country is lake area. There are over 50,000 lakes and 30,000 offshore islands.

Finland is divided into 12 provinces or counties with 78 urban municipalities (49 cities and 29 small towns) and 443 rural communes. It has the highest proportion of university students to population in the world. The five major cities are Helsinki (532,000), Tampere (153,000), Turku (152,000), Lahti (87,000), and Oulu (85,000). Four others have populations over 50,000: Pori, Kuopio, Jyväskylä, and Vaasa. Finland's cities and towns cover 1.6 percent of its land area. Of the population, 60 percent dwell in towns and urban districts; 40 percent in rural areas. Finnish is the language of 93.5 percent of the people; Swedish, of 6.5 percent. The religious affiliation of 93.1 percent of the people is the Lutheran church.

The farms, mostly under 25 acres, occupy 9 percent of the land. Snow covers the ground in the south from December to April, the north from November to May. A third of the country lies above the Arctic Circle. Visually the major part of the country looks like the State of Maine.

About 35 percent of the population works in industry, 32 percent in agriculture, and the rest in other occupations. In 1965 its exports totaled $1.43 billion and its imports $.27 billion. Its main trade is with Great Britain, Russia, West Germany, Sweden, the United States, Holland, and France. The main exports are wood and paper products, metal products, and some agricultural products. Finland's Democratic form of government has deep roots. A Diet of Four Estates was set up in 1634. In 1906, a one-chamber Parliament was created. Finland declared herself independent on December 6, 1917, and became a republic in July 1919. Its President serves a six-year term. The Parliament consists of 200 members chosen in an open election. The members of Parliament serve four-year terms. The political makeup of the Parliament is (1966–1960) one-quarter Socialist, one-quarter Center, one-quarter Peoples' Democrats (mainly Communists), and one-quarter a mixture of Conservatives, Liberals, Swedish, and others.

In 1968, there were 94 daily newspapers and 130 local papers in Finland. The circulation of all daily newspapers totaled 2,200,000.

The Finnish Currency unit is the *markka* (mark, Fmk). At the beginning of 1963, the monetary unit was changed with the introduction of a new mark, which is equivalent to 100 old marks. The Finnish *markka* was devalued by 23.8 percent on October 12, 1967. After devaluation, the exchange rate became U.S. $1.00 = 4.20 Fmks.

And so to the story of Tapiola.

68.
Finland.

69.
Cities and provinces.

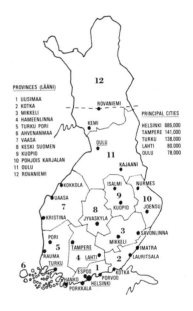

PROVINCES (LÄÄNI)

1 UUSIMAA
2 KOTKA
3 MIKKELI
4 HAMEENLINNA
5 TURKU PORI
6 AHVENANMAA
7 VAASA
8 KESKI SUOMEN
9 KUOPIO
10 POHJOIS KARJALAN
11 OULU
12 ROVANIEMI

PRINCIPAL CITIES

HELSINKI 686,000
TAMPERE 141,000
TURKU 138,000
LAHTI 80,000
OULU 78,000

70.
Roads and ferries.
71.
Railroads and ferries.

72.
Air routes.
73.
Mean annual temperature,
C°.

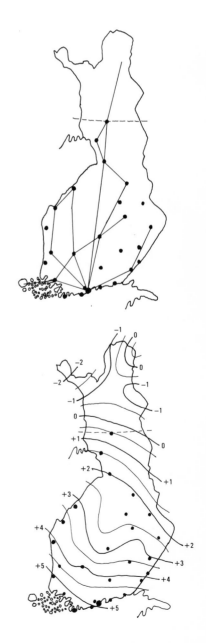

3 Building
Tapiola

Starting

At the end of World War II, Finland found itself in a state of economic and social chaos, as did most of the countries that had been in the war. The problems of wartime shortages were compounded by nearly half a million refugees. Extreme pressures for housing pointed to expedient objectives—such as providing a statistically specified number of rooms or apartments. In spite of extensive concern and discussion over the housing issue, there was little action. There was, moreover, little in the way of example to suggest solutions.

In my (H. von H.) capacity as a lawyer and director of a commercial bank in the biggest industrial town in Finland, Tampere, I became highly concerned with the everyday economic and social difficulties of the ordinary man and his family. I began writing newspaper articles about these matters and before long became Managing Director of the Finnish Family Welfare League (Väestöliitto), then one of Finland's most important social organizations. From social and family welfare I progressed to housing, for that is a key to solving most social problems. After extensive journeys through Finland and other Scandinavian countries I published a brief book—more accurately a pamphlet—called ''Koti vaiko kasarmi'' (Homes or Barracks).* In this book the idea of single-purpose housing was contrasted with the idea of full-range communities. The book tried to show that the difference between merely putting roofs over people's heads and providing them with viable multifaceted commu-

* Heikki von Hertzen, *Koti vaiko kasarmi lapsillemme*, Porvoo: (WSOY) 1946.

nities lay in basic intentions, in intelligent planning, and in effective execution. Narrowly conceived housing, in fact, could cause social pathology with such symptoms as malaise, indifference, crime, and vandalism. A real community-building effort, on the other hand, could produce an environment conducive to healthful social interchange and personal enrichment for persons of all ages and all interests.

In ''Homes or Barracks'' several good examples were highlighted. One was Käpylä, in Helsinki, then almost a quarter-century old. Käpylä combined good site planning with a simple rustic architecture. Another good example was the row houses composing ''Friluftsstaden'' (Open Air City) in Malmö, Sweden, built in 1944. Here small but carefully designed row houses had their own small gardens, each of which opened into a neighborhood common space. This was modern housing with a sense of community. The book also mentioned Radburn, New Jersey, which exemplified these principles as well as the idea of traffic separation between pedestrians and vehicles. Greenbelt, Maryland, was shown as an example of a whole town built on the Radburn principle.

These accomplishments shared one major feature: their basic objectives. These objectives were not ''to house so many people,'' ''develop so much residential land,'' or ''create so much construction employment'' but to create socially, biologically, and physically healthful environments. Further, this meant individuality as well as proximity of nature. Nature is a vital compo-

1.
The Tapiola site in relation
to Helsinki.
2.
The first houses in Tapiola;
one-family prefabricated
houses built by Puurakenne
Oy, a prefabrication firm.

nent of healthful town life, and the general quality of natural surroundings should be preserved as much as possible. All other objectives, as well as means, were secondary to these ends.

"Homes or Barracks" reached a large audience. It also revealed that neither those responsible for social policy nor most planners had satisfactory answers for handling Finland's planning or housing needs. People sought better and roomier dwellings, space for the young, and playgrounds for children. People wanted fresh air to breathe. They needed good surroundings and good services in residential areas. These were just as important as their dwellings. The book aroused much argument, which extended over a period of five years. But the end result was nil. Those, like myself, who wanted to revitalize town planning kept hearing the same answer—that *we* were utopians who meant well but whose ideas could not be realized. We were also told that only experienced local civil servants and building contractors understood the seemingly iron laws of economics regarding housing and town planning. We were told that it was not possible to do anything but continue along the same old lines.

Because we knew that this argument was wrong, our only course was to prove it to be wrong. We who believed that new town planning methods could be created decided to begin building a new town ourselves. To do this we had to go to a site outside Helsinki in order to have freedom in our planning and in order to avoid the stifling arm of bureaucracy—always the worst enemy of creative work and reform.

3.
The plan for Hagalund by
Otto-I. Meurman, dated
1945. Several distinct
neighborhoods are
indicated. The plan implies
a low proportion of
automobile ownership.
House sites are located on
local service streets, which
are distinct from
through-traffic roads.

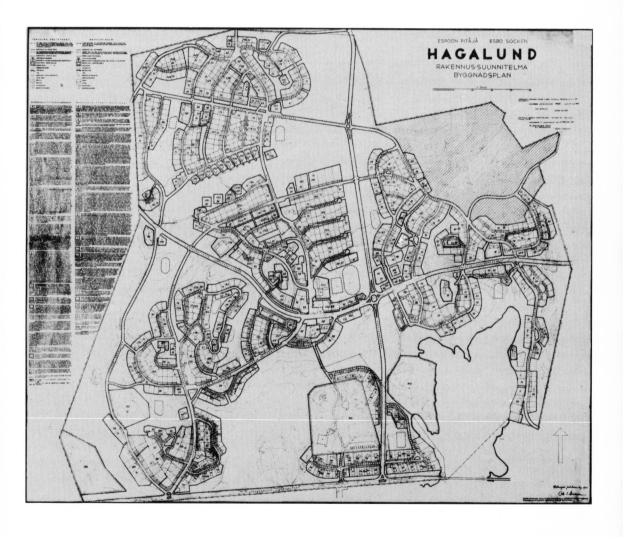

Financing a Complete Town
from the Beginning

Six miles west of Helsinki, beautifully located on
an inlet of the Gulf of Finland, was a tract of
660 acres of deeply wooded land. It was a per-
fect site for building an experimental new town
and to show what good planning could do. In-
terestingly enough, this site had been designated for development in Eliel Saarinen's plan
for greater Helsinki, drawn in 1918. In the mid-
1940s, it had been planned as a group of four
residential neighborhoods by Otto-I. Meurman.
Our aim was to realize Meurman's plan, but as
a whole community, not just a dormitory. The
land cost was very high, in relation to the Finnish circumstances very high indeed. A large
sum was needed, and quickly.

I first learned of this site in the year 1950. A
number of contractors were already bidding for
it in bits and pieces. Had it been sold piecemeal,
it would have been totally despoiled. Moreover,
at that time no bank in Finland was inclined to
underwrite the kind of project we had in mind.
The bankers admitted that our ideas were interesting, even exciting, but too utopian. They
also felt that the land price was exorbitantly
high. (However, five years later in 1955, they
felt that I had gotten the land ''for nothing.'' I
could not resist replying how useful it would
have been had they held that opinion in 1950.)
The Finnish Government, although eager to procure new housing for some 425,000 displaced
Finns, could not offer any help at this stage.
Government funds were low after paying our
huge war reparations. For a while it seemed almost certain that the idea of creating a new

town would remain but a fleeting dream, like so
many similar and previous projects all over the
world. But I would not give up easily.

So it was that an attack on the financial problem was approached from several directions.
Two early attempts ended in failure. The first
was an offer put before the Sales Association for
Prefabricated Houses (Myyntiyhdistys Puutalo),
an organization that represents Finland's leading
wood processing industries. The necessary capital could not be released. The second attempt
was directed to the National Pensions Institute.
They, in fact, had the necessary capital, but they
were interested in investing in land only—not in
creating a new town.

I then realized that a rather specially consti-
tuted body was required to get things going. It
could not be done by normal private enterprise
whose purpose is, after all, to make a maximum
profit. Nor could it be done by an existing public
agency that could not be geared to the likely
complexities and needed skills. Something between the two was required, something that
would have the flexibility and freedom of action
of a private company but, at the same time, the
power and influence of a public authority. What
was needed was a foundation with powerful social and political backing. And it would have to
be able to operate dynamically like a private
company.

Before such an organization could be created, a vital move had to be made. The ownership of the 660 acres had to be secured. Without that any venture would be fantasy. There was no choice but to stop talking and start doing.

At that moment, as managing director of the Finnish Family Welfare League, I persuaded my organization to involve itself in community planning and building. I told my Board that it could not expect progress in social and family welfare without good housing. Nor, I said, could there be decent housing without good town planning. The immediate problem was money— specifically, money to buy the 660-acre Hagalund estate. The price was 180 million old Finnish Marks (then about $563,000.00). The interest rate was 7½ percent* and interest and a discount payment would be added to the purchase price.

At that time the Finnish Family Welfare League had nowhere near this amount. However, I persuaded the Family Welfare League to countersign a banker's draft for two months as part of a wider strategy to arouse greater interest. This also quieted the criticism that the idea was idle utopianism. More pressing was the anxiety of the Board of the Family Welfare League to know just what would happen in two months when the banker's draft would come due. Thus it fell upon me to set in motion a chain of actions during the first and most difficult period, the next eighteen

* Here and throughout, all costs are stated as of the time of the transaction:

$1.00 = 4.20 Finnish Marks (Fmk) since October 14, 1967
$1.00 = 3.20 Fmk prior to October 14, 1967 (1 Fmk = 100 Old Fmk)

Note also that a square meter equals 10.764 square feet.

months. I first succeeded in convincing the seller (Hagalund was then owned in its entirety by Dr. Arne Grahn) to accept terms under which we were to pay only 50 percent of the price in cash. The rest was to be paid in two installments on January 31, 1952, and on January 31, 1953. The banks were still not prepared to back us, but I nevertheless succeeded in getting our first banker's draft from a temporary fund, held by various social organizations.

Due to certain circumstances they could lend the money for only two months. So through still other agreements I secured a second banker's draft to be available in two months' time. This second draft was granted as a three-month loan from the State Football Pool, which often has large sums to lend for short periods. The value of Hagalund was thus underwritten a second time. The Football Pool was willing to lend money on the Hagalund site because they were fully aware of the site's value; they had nothing to lose. But all this was still a temporary expedient. Further preparatory agreements were made to assure smooth operations with even more short-term credits. Of course, a long-term loan remained the real goal.

The time was now ripe for the Family Welfare League to make its decisive move. On July 31, 1951, Mr. V. J. Sukselainen, the President of the League, and I signed a contract of sale under which the Family Welfare League bought Hagalund from Dr. Arne Grahn at a price of 180 million old Finnish marks.

The negotiations had taken eight months and had been exhausting. Twenty separate drafts for the Contract of Sale had been prepared and discarded. The twenty-first draft was accepted and signed, with great hesitation, by Dr. Grahn. As soon as the contract was signed, I left Helsinki, totally exhausted. A two weeks' holiday in Lapland and on the gigantic Norwegian fiords along the Arctic Ocean restored me. Never in my life had I been so in need of a good rest.

The next step was to obtain broader backing. I then convened a meeting of the directors of five other national organizations, similar in structure to the Family Welfare League. The choice of these five organizations was critical, for these organizations, together with the Family Welfare League, had to represent Finland's entire consumer range for housing. Even more important, they had to represent Finland's political spectrum. Another condition was that each of the organizations had to have leaders who were strong, independent, capable of making decisions, and authoritative.

The directors of the five organizations were assembled. I announced to them that the Family Welfare League had purchased the Hagalund estate and that it intended to build a new town there as a model community. The directors were told that from all the organizations in Finland we had selected them to participate in this venture, and we told them why. I admitted that we had a most difficult task ahead of us and that we had to start work with few resources, almost empty-handed. We were also burdened with a loan of 180 million old Finnish marks with an interest of 7½ percent. Because of the pressure of time I stated that we had to have their answers within

seven days—their answers as to whether they would participate jointly with us.

Within the seven days all five had agreed to join. On September 27, 1951, they signed the charter that created an organization called Asuntosäätiö (the Housing Foundation). The constituent organizations were

1. The Family Welfare League (Väestöliitto)
2. The Mannerheim League for Child Welfare
3. The Society of Civil Servants
4. The Confederation of Finnish Trade Unions
5. The Finnish Association of Disabled Veterans and Servicemen
6. The Central Association of Tenants

Politically, the first three are conservative, and the last three are socialist. Asuntosäätiö was to be the instrument that would build Tapiola. The next step was administrative. The Hagalund property was transferred from ownership by the Family Welfare League to Asuntosäätiö.

To succeed in the task that lay ahead, it was of utmost importance that the Board of Asuntosäätiö be made up of men with expert knowledge and influence, as well as the moral fortitude and idealism that would be needed. Within a few years these qualities were demonstrated. From 1951, when the Hagalund area was purchased, until 1956, when the income from the sales of the sites was beginning to balance Asuntosäätiö's outlay, the work had to be financed by short-term bank loans, some of them in the form of "bills of exchange." Naturally, they had to be renewed at regular intervals. At the beginning everything went relatively smoothly. The day arrived, however, when a serious message from one of the underwriting banks was delivered: a bill due in a few days' time could no longer be

renewed unless three board members of Asuntosäätiö gave their personal guarantees.

An emergency meeting of the Board was
called, and the facts were presented. There was
but a few seconds' silence. Then, the oldest
member of the board arose and said, "Tell those
bank gentlemen that we are not going to make
martyrs of some of the members of the board.
Tell them that the whole board will come to
countersign as a body at ten o'clock tomorrow
morning." And that, in fact, is what happened.
The unanimous group marched solemnly to the
bank's head office and signed a lengthy paper.
Before parting company we agreed, confiden-
tially, that we would not cause our wives sleep-
less nights by making mention of the matter.

This act made a considerable impression. The
building of Tapiola has proceeded since on normal banking lines and with increasing mutual
trust. The crisis further increased the feeling of
solidarity among the members of the board and
added to its power and influence. However, its
larger significance was that men who represented opposite spheres of interest and who held
divergent political views had found a common
aim worth fighting for.

It must be remembered that the building of Tapiola (which is now nearing the completion of its
housing) was financed by only one source of income. This was the income received from the
sale of sites. The price of sites included all the
costs: the capital invested in the land, which has
more than doubled in value over the last fifteen
years; all technical and engineering costs; and,
of course, all the planning and administrative expenses. Asuntosäätiö is probably unique in pos-

sessing the financial facts of what it really costs
to build a town for 20,000 people.

There are some rather interesting statistics on
the building costs in Tapiola during the first
three years of construction, compared with building costs in Finland as a whole. This is for the
period 1953 to 1955. The building cost of Tapiola's houses—including a proportionate cost of
the heating company, the heating system, the
commercial buildings, and the public facilities—
averaged $11.80 per square foot (Fmk 406.60
per square meter) from 1953 to 1955. The corresponding average for Finland as a whole for
building enterprises supported by secondary state
loans was $12.15 per square foot (Fmk 418.75
per square meter), 3 percent higher. It has been
possible to achieve this because of comprehensive planning and large-scale building.

Site Prices in Tapiola Although all costs were
included in the site prices, they have been deci-
sively lower than those within the boundaries of
Helsinki, just alongside Tapiola. When sites sold
in the open market in the suburb of Lauttassaari
(the part of Helsinki closest to Tapiola) were
bringing (in 1965) from $10.50 to $12.20 per
square foot (Fmk 360 to 420 per square meter),
the site price in Tapiola was $4.07 per square
foot (Fmk 140 square meter). Furthermore, this
price was charged by Asuntosäätiö for only one-
fifth of its sites, for those sold in the open market. Four-fifths of the sites were sold at a price
of $1.44 (Fmk 65) per dwelling square meter
(multistory buildings) or $1.55 (Fmk 70) per
dwelling square foot (row and town houses).* An

* In Finland the site prices are given as "so many mks per
inhabited dwelling sq.m.," not per site sq.m.

additional comparison can be made by mentioning that in the corresponding period the market price for sites within the whole urban area of Helsinki was between $8.85 and $15.90 per square foot (Fmk 400 to 720 per dwelling square meter). A site for a private house of 8,400 square feet (779 square meters) was sold at a price of $1,570.00 (Fmk 6,600). To make it quite clear, the price mentioned here means the total price for the site including municipal engineering.

Asuntosäätiö's policy of selling the sites for, in general, rather low prices and attracting the state-subsidized housing to Tapiola needs an explanation. Asuntosäätiö wanted to build everyman's town—not just a rich man's town that would prove little nor a workingman's district that ought to be a thing of the past. Asuntosäätiö wanted to have various kinds of people live, work, and thrive side by side in the same modern community, and their children would attend the same schools and participate in common activities. For this reason Asuntosäätiö wanted to obtain as much state-supported housing production as possible so as to put Tapiola within the reach of all citizens. With this in view, Asuntosäätiö sold 80 percent of its sites for long-term, low-interest ARAVA State loans for building. This was a heavy additional economic burden, since site prices approved by ARAVA were kept to a very low level. When Asuntosäätiö sold 80 percent of its plots for ARAVA financing, it sold 80 percent at a price that was only about half of its open-market value. This was a very great sacrifice made for the sake of achieving a real cross-section community.

The Financing of the Housing From 1953 to 1966 when most of the dwellings in Tapiola were built, the financing of the housing supported by the state was organized in the following way. The state granted a secondary loan with an interest rate of 1 percent. This loan covered 30 to 40 percent of the total cost (including cost of site) in the case of an occupier-owned house or an occupier-owned apartment. A rental house was usually granted a maximum loan of 50 percent of total cost. In addition, 40 to 50 percent could be obtained as a primary loan from the free capital market, from saving banks, insurance companies, and so forth, at 7½ to 8 percent. This left the residents themselves to find the remaining 15 to 20 percent, varying with the price of the house. The state loan would be amortized over 47 years.

As can be seen from the table the total building cost (inclusive of site) for a terrace house of five rooms and kitchen, 925 square feet (86 square meters), was $7,857.00 (Fmk 33,000). The actual price paid by the resident was $2,133.00 (Fmk 8,960). This was the amount of the owner capital to be invested by the buyer. Another example: a flat of three rooms and kitchen, completed in 1964, cost $10,207.00, and the needed equity capital was $2,324.00. Among the buyers of this type of dwelling are people like carpenters, electrical fitters, pipe fitters, telegraph clerks, detectives, watchmakers, warehousemen, postmen, and clerks. The owner capital needed was collected during a period of three to four years with the help of the "saving-for-housing" system, established by Asuntosäätiö in cooperation with some big commercial and saving banks.

Housing Company	Year Completed	Type of Dwelling[2]	Area		Total building cost of the apartment[3]	Owner equity or capital
			M²	Ft²		
Kontiontie	1955	5 r + k	86	925	$ 7,857	$2,133
Miilupolku	1958	3 r + k	65	700	7,776	2,052
Riistapolku	1960	2 r + k	56	602	6,933	1,791
Sudenkorento	1961	4 r + k	94.5	1020	11,414	3,270
Louhenkallio	1964	3 r + k	70	752	10,207	2,324
Louhentalo[1]	1964	2 r + k	54	580	10,079	8,566
One-family house (Järvi type)	1967	4 r+k+s+c	81	870	8,905	3,786

[1] Non-ARAVA, not subsidized by the state
[2] r = room, k = kitchen, s = sauna bath, c = cellar
[3] Rate of exchange $ 1.00 = 4.20 Finnish marks (Fmk)

It might be of some interest to make a comparison between the two housing groups called Louhenkallio and Louhentalo, both completed in 1964. Louhenkallio is a normal ARAVA building, subsidized by the state, in contrast to Louhentalo, which is non-ARAVA (not subsidized). With $2,324.00, one could buy a three-room flat (70 square meters) in Louhenkallio, whereas one had to pay $8,566.00 for a two-room flat (54 square meters) in Louhentalo. The total building cost for both flats was about the same, roughly $10,000. Here the influence of the state subsidies in the purchasing cost of the dwelling (to the amount of owner capital) can clearly be seen. With the help of the subsidies the purchase and ownership of a dwelling was made possible even for low- and middle-income people. As already mentioned, the "saving-for-housing" system has effectively supported this policy.

In 1965, Asuntosäätiö published a booklet on the sale cost of dwellings, down payments, average rent returns, and site prices in Tapiola from 1954 to 1965. The effect of this booklet on public opinion was considerable. The press, however, remained aloof and did not comment.

Financing of the Municipal Engineering Costs
Public utilities in Finland are usually constructed by municipalities and financed from interest-free tax funds. In Tapiola, however, a completely new town had to build up from scratch. Asuntosäätiö was responsible for everything, including public utilities. The costs had to be paid back through receipts from sales of land and buildings. Ordinarily, the site improvement and utility costs are financed by short-term credits, usually

at 8 percent interest. Our problem was at the time that no bank in Finland would lend money for this purpose. The difficulty was settled when the State Postal Savings Bank extended our first medium-term loan. This was a five-year loan for about $167,000.00 (50 million old Fmks) at 7½ percent interest. This took place at the end of 1952. We used the money to pay the municipal engineering costs in the first neighborhood (streets, roads, water pipes, sewage, storm sewers, street lighting, etc.) The first occupants moved in two and a half years later. By the time the first neighborhood was completed for occupancy, this sum was used up. Income from the sales of the sites of the houses in the first neighborhood were the first earnings Asuntosäätiö received. These were plowed right back so as to continue the work.

Our first long-term credit was obtained in 1953. This loan was for $312,000.00 (100 million old Fmks) for 13 years at 3 percent interest. It came from the State Accounting Office. The last major loan was not to be procured until 1957, by which time Tapiola could show concrete accomplishments. The maximum amount of long-term credits was $940,000.00 (300 million old Fmks). At this writing (1969), all the money has been paid back except a small part of the last loan, which will be paid in 1970. Thus, a period of 18 years spans the creation of a new town and its financing from start to finish.

Programming, Planning, and Building

In 1951, when Asuntosäätiö bought the Hagalund estate, it became heir to the plan drawn by
Professor Otto-I. Meurman in 1945 for this area.
This plan had been approved officially and thus
had legal status. It was clear from the outset
that far-reaching modifications would have to be
made in this plan, but it was a sufficient basis
for getting started. Nevertheless, Professor
Meurman's plan proved to be very important for
the planning of Tapiola as a whole, even though
the final solution differs substantially from the
original. Work began in 1952 under the direction of Asuntosäätiö. The water supply problems
of the future community had to be settled first.
This planning work was commissioned by Asuntosäätiö to Mr. Eino Kajaste, Chief Engineer of
the Helsinki city waterworks. The waste treatment system was planned by Mr. Paavo Hyö-
mäki, Chief Engineer, also commissioned by
Asuntosäätiö. The preparation of a plan for surface drainage was also begun in this phase.

Engineering reports indicated that the water
supply would have to come via Otaniemi from
the network of Helsinki and that the most suitable place for the sewage filtering plant was a
field in the immediate vicinity of Hagalund radio
station. Most of the sewage system was to work
on the gravity pipe principle. These facts, together with related economic considerations,
pointed to starting in the eastern neighborhood
of Tapiola.

Today, few can imagine what it meant to plan
a community in the early 1950s, when all the
fundamental data were missing. There was no
adequate map, nor were there population and
traffic projections. Wherever we turned for ad-
vice, the answer was always the same: "Sorry,
I haven't the faintest idea." In every respect,
planning had to be started in Tapiola from a
base of absolutely nothing, with one essential
exception—Meurman's plan.

The first important decision was to coordinate
very closely the following factors: site planning,
site engineering components (roads, water,
sewer, storm drains), and architectural design. At
the same time it was vital to strive constantly for
the economically best solutions. The buildings
were, naturally, sited to give the optimal cost solution. The streets, water pipes, sewage, and
culverts, too, were planned to be as economical
as possible. However, these aspects were not
achieved independently of each other. The deciding factor was the overall result—the sum
total of the building costs and the civil engineering costs. This total sum was to be as low
as possible. This meant, in practice, that it was
sometimes necessary to make do with only the
third cheapest municipal engineering solution if
it yielded a decisive saving on the building side
of the ledger. This method of procedure was, at
the time and to the best of my knowledge, completely new in Finland. But the results soon
began to provide the justification.

The modifications of Meurman's plan are important to mention. In his site plan Meurman
had proposed a low-density crossroads village.
His plan of about 740 houses and a few large
buildings—and estimating four to five persons
per household—meant a population of from
3,000 to 4,000. This, in turn, added up to a
population density of only six persons per acre
(a third of a typical American suburb). Asunto-

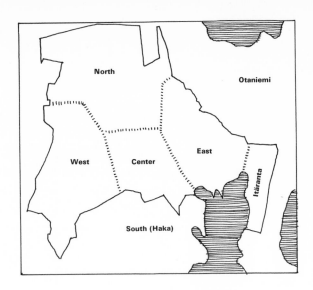

säätiö had a considerably higher figure in mind: 30 persons per acre, by no means an arbitrary number. It had been arrived at as a result of careful observation of previous developments. It would allow a high level of public services without overcrowding and would mean a more economical apportionment for the eventual payment of the land cost. The main reason for the density selected, however, remained the conviction that it was the most satisfactory in terms of the social objectives in view, namely, a real town with all the social, commercial, and leisure facilities that people need. The successful realization of these objectives was much more than a matter of statistics, however. An essential corollary was good physical design.

Good design was the obvious next step in a sequence that had thus far achieved (a) initial financing; (b) political support; (c) adequate and well-located site; (d) an opportunity for competition with accepted development forms; and, not least, (e) a working instrument for creating the new town, namely, Asuntosäätiö.

It should also be remembered that help had not yet come from the government, local or national. Asuntosäätiö's creation, Tapiola, was to be built for all practical purposes by private enterprise on the same competitive terms as any other enterprise in Finland. The degree of Asuntosäätiö's self-reliance is indicated by the fact that the local community was unwilling to provide roads, sewers, or waterlines. Asuntosäätiö had to finance that itself. Only primary schools and some other services could get funds from municipal tax revenues. From the competitive angle, Tapiola may even be said to have been slightly handicapped.

The First or Eastern Neighborhood Our principal task at this point (1952) was to find some good architects. Alvar Aalto was too busy, but Aarne Ervi, Viljo Revell, Aulis Blomstedt, and Markus Tavio were available. They were architects of experience, taste, reputation, and recognition. The four formed a team to design the buildings of the first phase of the first neighborhood. The actual site design for the first neighborhood was done by this team, based on Meurman's original plan. Meurman has proposed four neighborhoods separated by green belts, the town to be divided into quadrants by two crossing roads, one east-west, one north-south. This we considered a serious shortcoming for the future planning, for at our higher density heavy through traffic would cut the town into four isolated parts and prevent it from working as a well-planned entity. Meurman's plan had established a high standard of design for the years immediately following World War II, that is, the era previous to automobile dominance. The four neighborhoods that Meurman proposed, nevertheless, had a useful developmental as well as a social rationale for our purposes. They were convenient and reasonable entities to develop in the face of then-existing conditions, each neighborhood having its own related shops and services. But something obviously would have to be done about the crossing roads. That was to occur later.

The architects of the first neighborhood were to design buildings suited to the terrain, to develop a site plan, and to conceive the character of the overall environment. Naturally, they had to work in close cooperation with the technical team and the housing team appointed by the board of Asuntosäätiö and to submit their work for review by these teams. The work of each architect was thoroughly evaluated by the housing team. The members of the team consisted of two independent architects, a building engineer, a heating engineer, an electrical engineer, a landscape gardener, a domestic science expert, a child welfare expert, a sociologist, and, not least, a practical-minded housewife. This team assessed the overall as well as the detailed design of the houses. The housing team that performed the programming of the planning, together with the board of Asuntosäätiö, represented housing applicants from all classes. The locale of the first neighborhood, determined by utility location, was in the northeast quadrant. It was also slightly hilly, in other words, quite suited to residential use.

At this point several important decisions on the part of Asuntosäätiö had become necessary. First, there was the commitment to an overall planning concept, reasonably flexible, yet with a direction: neighborhoods connected rather than separated by open spaces, and separation of pedestrian-vehicular circulation. Second was the decision to use the best architects, engineers, landscape architects, and other experts available, an idea that requires little justification. Third was the decision to provide the community facilities that would establish a real basis for personal interaction, for real community. This meant, for example, an elementary school, a movie theater, and a shopping center that also served as a community center, albeit a modest one. All had to be built from the start as part of the first neighborhood. The community center had a restaurant-cafe from the very beginning, a place where people could meet at leisure. It also meant giving the occupants power of decision in community matters. Fourth, there was the decision to build a variety of types of dwellings and to build them near one another, thus assuring an integration of family types and age groups rather than their separation. It also meant a more flexible community composition and, most important, diversification of income classes.

All in all, these early commitments embody the objectives that have pervaded Tapiola's creation. These derive from the intention to build a town for everyone, not an affluent upper-class town or a subsidized lower-class town. It is relatively easy to build for one class or another and extremely hard, but essential, to build a real cross-section community—a vital attribute of a genuine new towns effort. A real cross-section population is the essence of a real city, and anything less makes it that much less of a city. The commitment to establish a real community is evidenced by Asuntosäätiö's insistence on providing all of the elements that constitute community. These are four: (1) housing, with a great variety of types; (2) services, from shopping to medical care to schools; (3) work, from blue-collar to white-collar jobs; and (4) recreation, from outdoor sports to indoor theater.

Asuntosäätiö proved its commitments to these objectives at its earliest opportunity, in the creation of the first neighborhood. Roads and utilities were built and house construction started in 1952. In the fall of 1953, the first inhabitants moved in. By 1956, the first neighborhood was complete.

In the construction of the first neighborhood Asuntosäätiö learned some important lessons in community design, in effect, ways of translating social objectives into brick and mortar. For example, to ensure that a particular area be mixed socially, it is necessary to provide different types of dwellings in close proximity. This may mean row houses near high-rise buildings, apartments near single houses, walk-ups near semidetached houses. This, in turn, means a problem of architectural compatibility.

The usual course is to make an administrative decision. For instance, if development portion "x" is to have so many apartments and so many row houses, simply commission one architect to design the apartment buildings and another to design the rows. Supposedly the variety will enrich the visual scene. This is a seriously mistaken notion. Most likely, the result will be two types of buildings in proximity but not in harmony, causing awkwardness and an overemphasis of their differences. What started as a good intention becomes a clumsy juxtaposition. While most city streets house a myriad of diverse and complementary functions, their architecture serves the essential function of conjoining these separate functions in the viewer's eye and mind.

To achieve the same effect in a new group of buildings in nature, it is much wiser to assign architects to groups of different buildings rather than single types of buildings. Consequently the commissioning agency must subdivide a site into developmental entities that are also social as well as design entities. Probably a staff architect or consulting architect should be given this administrative responsibility, but it can also be done by an architectural team. The point, then, is that the administration of a new town must program its development portions as social, economic, construction, and design entities. In fact, this should impose no burden. It is not only good sense but a positive advantage in administrative operations. A still more fundamental point is that good architectural design does not happen by itself. The necessary conditions must be created before an architect begins his design assignment. This holds equally true for the most talented architects available. Essentially the conditions of good architectural design are sound social objectives, a construction schedule, a community plan, and a site plan. The last is an embodiment of the other factors.

To illustrate the necessity of this kind of administrative responsibility, one might consider how one of Asuntosäätiö's chief objectives was realized, that is, achieving a physical mixture of different social and economic classes.

This objective was realized in the building of one of Tapiola's very first group of houses, designed by Aulis Blomsted. These were semidetached (''weak link'' in Finnish architects' terminology) and related to adjoining four-story walk-ups. Both designs were for spacious, handsomely detailed, and well-outfitted dwellings—and their intended customers materialized quickly. Within forty yards of the semidetached houses, running parallel on slightly higher ground, low apartment houses were built for people of more modest means. These were designed by the same architect. It was of the highest order of importance that the two types of architecture not only harmonize but indeed complement each other. This meant a kinship in materials, details, fenestration, facade, and relationship to sky and soil. On a city street the job of relationships might not be too difficult or critical, dominated with buildings as that visual scene is. But on a natural open site, where the natural scene furnishes the basic visual tone, the relationship between architectural elements is crucial and delicate. It really was a matter of the utmost design skill, because the first inhabitants—the upper-class middle-income people—could not be deceived. Of necessity their confidence had to be earned, first through promise, then through fulfillment. This was an essential step toward attracting buyers of all classes to Tapiola. Not only is this a matter of building group design but of site design, one of administration's most sensitive responsibilities. For example, various roads connect Tapiola's schools with its neighborhood shopping groups. These roads pass through numerous residential areas. The roads, or sometimes paths, obviously become the locales of casual meeting.

These subtle fundamentals are demonstrated further in another subsection of the first neighborhood with a row of five handsome high-income houses. They are stark by American standards but quietly elegant through proportion, materials, and massing by Finnish standards. They are one story in height. Running parallel is a group of two-story wooden houses, which are among the lowest-cost houses in Tapiola. Both groups, the cheapest and the most expensive, are designed by the same architects, Kaija and Heikki Siren. The westward side, facing affluent neighbors, has small rectilinear gardens, just the ''right'' size for a busy man's family. These gardens are ample enough to be useful but not so large as to become a maintenance nuisance. The result is that the small private gardens serve as buffers, visually and acoustically. Again a common path to common neighborhood facilities is shared between the two types of houses.

In both examples mentioned, the juxtaposition of the grander houses with their more modest neighbors was achieved without awkward over-emphasis but rather through highly skilled site planning and architecture. It was completely unselfconscious. The private view of both houses was westward, for Finland's winter evening sun. The view of the more modest dwellings was to the conjoining common or shared public space. Also, they were higher to afford a better view. The ''richer'' houses enjoyed a more private view, which included a large vista of uninterrupted natural scenery. The common space was maintained by Asuntosäätiö's landscaping and grounds department.

4.
Site plan of the eastern
neighborhood. This was
built in two phases—the
first is the upper portion,
the second the lower
portion beneath the slightly
curved east-west road.

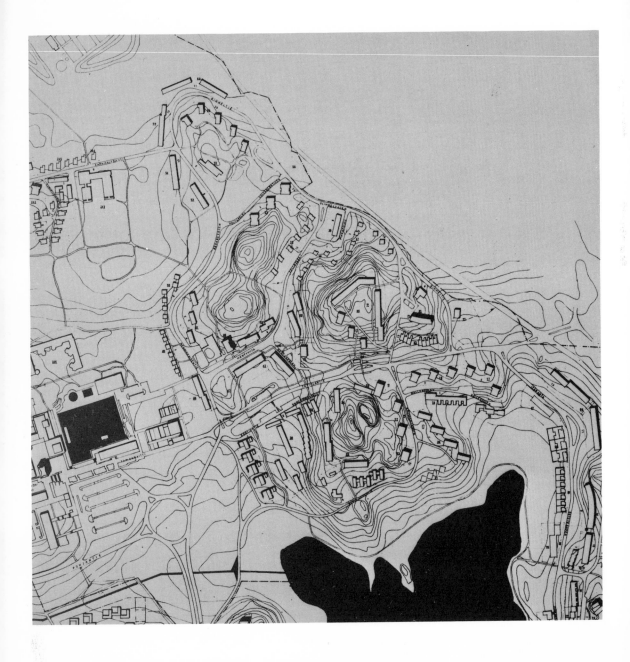

5.
Model of the first phase of
the eastern neighborhood.

The Eastern Neighborhood 88-89

6.
Air view of "Phase 1" of
the eastern neighborhood,
looking due south toward
the archipelago. This is a
late photograph, and it
shows the tower of the
town center and, to the
right, part of the western
neighborhood.

7.
Air view of "Phase 2" of
the eastern neighborhood,
looking due north. The
stack of the first central
heating plant can be seen at
the left. Otaniemi is to the
right.

8.
Five-story apartment houses
built as part of ''Phase 1.''
They were designed for
young families with small
children by Marcus Tavio.

10.
The eastern neighborhood
center during the Christmas
season. (foto Atte
Matilainen)
11.
Study model of the
community center of the
eastern neighborhood.

12.
Floor plan of the
eleven-story tower that
marks the center of
Tapiola's first (eastern)
neighborhood. These were
"efficiency" apartments
ranging in size from 344 to
484 square feet. Architect,
Arne Ervi. (scale 1:220)

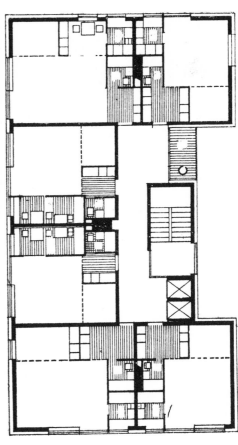

13a,b,c.
Some of the outdoor
recreational activities in
Tapiola.

14.
The "weak-link" houses in the eastern neighborhood, designed by Aulis Blomsted. The direction of view is out toward nature facing westward. Note the pool of ground water at the upper left.

15.
The weak-link houses seen from the west, with the higher houses behind. The pool of ground water has become a play pool for children.

16.
An early view of the
weak-link houses. The
gardens are provided for
apartment dwellers.
17.
The view westward from the
weak-link houses.

18.
The weak-link houses in
winter.

19.
The "Ketju" weak-link or
semidetached houses,
designed by Aulis Blomsted,
1954. (scale, about 1:220+)

20.
Multistory flats to the rear
of the weak-link houses.
Four-room units with
kitchens measure 936
square feet; two-room units
with kitchenette measure
603 square feet. Architect,
Aulis Blomsted. (scale,
about 1:220+)

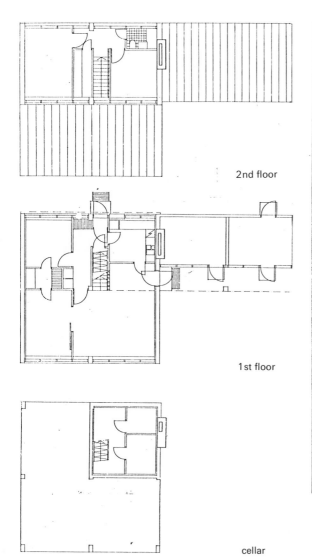

2nd floor

1st floor

cellar

21.
The two-story wood prefab
houses, designed by Kaija
and Heikki Siren. Note the
size of the gardens.
22.
Plan of the two-story
prefabs.

23.
Landscaping between the
row houses.
24.
The relationship between
two rather different income
groups in Tapiola. The front
houses are for the more
affluent; the ones just
behind are the two-story
prefabs. This view is taken
looking due east. Helsinki's
skyline is on the horizon.

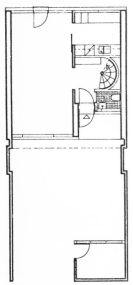

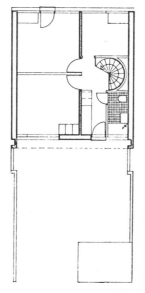

25.
A portion of "Phase 2" of
the eastern neighborhood,
in model form. This area
lies alongside Otsolahti Bay.
The toothlike houses in the
center are for artists.
26.
Artist's houses in Tapiola.
They are owned by the
Finnish Society of Artists
and leased for five-year
periods. There are some
large studios for big
commissions.

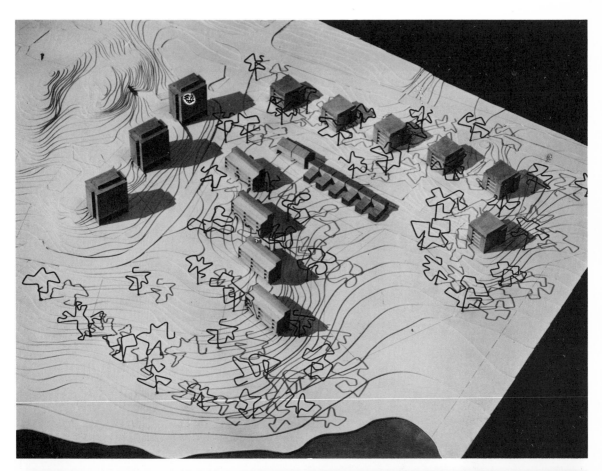

27.
Air view of the southern
portion of ''Phase 2,''
looking westward to the
town center. The six
four-story walk-up houses in
the right foreground were
designed by Esko Suhonen.

28.
Four-story walk-up houses
designed by Esko Suhonen.
Three rooms plus kitchen
and dining area measure
742 square feet; two rooms
plus kitchen and dining area
measure 489 square feet.
(scale about 1:220+).

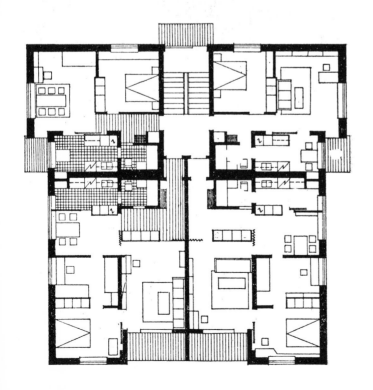

29.
Children in Tapiola.

30.
More children in
Tapiola—during the annual
community cleanup.

31.
Flowers in Tapiola.

32.
More flowers in Tapiola.

33.
The Otsonpesä terrace
houses designed by Kaija
and Heikki Siren, 1959.
Plan. North, up.

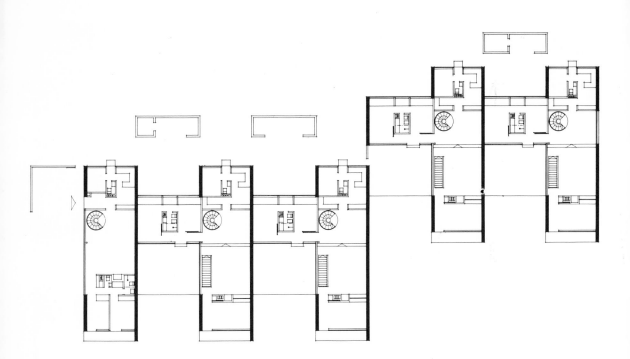

34.
Interior view of an
Otsonpesä terrace house.
35.
The Otsonpesä terrace
houses, designed by Kaija
and Heikki Siren, 1959.
They are in the southern
portion of the eastern
neighborhood, near
Otsolahti Bay.

36.
The Otsonpesä row houses
in winter. Note how the
areas of dark woodwork
form a pattern with the
white of the snow and the
white of the brick walls.

North

Otaniemi

West   Center   East

Itäranta

South (Haka)

The Town Center The goal in building Tapiola was to create a thriving, self-contained community. A basic requirement was that it should have a versatile business, administrative, and cultural center. This would have to satisfy the leisure-time, cultural, and social needs of the inhabitants as fully as possible.

On November 21, 1953, Asuntosäätiö announced a competition for Finnish architects to plan the center of Tapiola and its immediate surroundings. The announcement stated that the competition offered Finnish architects an opportunity in town planning that had rarely been provided before in Finland and would not occur often during the lifetime of one generation. The competition entries were judged on June 9, 1954, and aroused great attention. It was won by Aarne Ervi and his associates, and he was awarded the commission to plan the town center. The second prize went to Veikko Malmio, and the third to Osmo Sipari. The proposals of Kaija and Heikki Siren, Jorma Järvi, and Viljo Revell also won acclaim. Through this competition Asuntosäätiö found an excellent planner for the center of Tapiola. Moreover, Asuntosäätiö had also identified architects in Finland who had matured to the status of community planners by the early 1950s. Professor Otto-I. Meurman, a member of the jury, remarked that the competition entries were of a very high standard and that the results were very mature.

By 1968, a number of buildings had been completed in the center of Tapiola:
1. The central administrative tower ("Keskustorni"), Tapiola's landmark. It has a restaurant and terrace cafe on top. The top portion is also a beacon of light, which identifies Tapiola at night, even from considerable distances.
2. The shopping center and its complement called "Heikintori." This is a combined department store, consisting of fifty specialty shops and a social center. It has the first shopping arcade built in Finland, a covered shopping street that also offers numerous facilities for day and evening activities. It also houses high-class specialty shops and services. These include a tourist center and meeting hall, a spacious cafe for young people, a discotheque, premises for leisure-time activities and evening classes, restaurants, cafeterias, coffee bars, and kiosks that are open until late in the evening.
3. Alongside the artificial pool, which dominates the town center, stands the church with its parish hall and youth center, the swimming pool with ancillary outdoor facilities, and the health center with doctor's offices, clinics, and laboratories. There is also a sports hall with a bowling alley, a physical fitness school, and a gymnasium.
4. Plans have been completed for an international tourist hotel with restaurants as well as banqueting and congress halls on the southern side of the pool. A theater and a concert hall as well as a library and a college of music have been planned for the area between the western side of the pool and the central tower "Keskustorni." Future plans also include an exhibition hall for fine arts. All these facilities are concrete examples of the differences between a whole-

somely planned community and a dormitory town.

In his prize-winning plan Ervi showed great ingenuity in converting liabilities into assets. One of the problems was an ugly gravel pit on the site of the future town center. Ervi proposed turning this liability into an asset by converting it into a reflecting pool. Around the pool the above-mentioned facilities were envisioned in conceptual form. Ervi's design suggested that a population of 20,000 might be insufficient for serving all the cultural, commercial, and recreational needs of a modern urban inhabitant. In various later stages of design, Tapiola's town center was to be enlarged, to the point where it will eventually serve the future of its surrounding areas. This future population will, one day, amount to 80,000 persons. Meanwhile, Tapiola would be, in part, a functional satellite of Helsinki, but that was never taken to mean that it could not enjoy any or all of the activities found in Helsinki. In Ervi's competition plan, however, certain inadequacies in Professor Meurman's original plan began to be resolved.

Meurman had conceived of a low-density village. Traffic in the 1940s was not a particularly serious issue. Taken in the context of post-World War II Finland, his supposition was entirely tenable. While events do not support attributes of farsightedness in his plan, neither does retrospect disdain it as unreasonable. As it was, a town center serving 80,000 in a town of 20,000 residents meant a reappraisal of the original traffic plan. Clearly, the original crossroads system needed correction. Ervi proposed that the two crossroads be partly relocated and, in some places, eliminated. The east-west

component would be shifted south, and the upper portion of the north-south road eliminated. This meant that Tapiola's road system would penetrate from outside to inside but would not traverse the town. Traffic would serve but not dominate.

In principle, one of the functions of Meurman's road system was to link the neighborhoods together. At low densities this would have worked. They could still serve this end for higher densities, in Ervi's view, if they became pedestrian rather than vehicular pathways. Thus, it was not so much their abandonment that Ervi introduced as their readaptation. In fact, Tapiola has several circulation systems: the vehicular system, a bicycle system, and a pedestrian system.

There is an important lesson to be learned from the process of altering Tapiola's plan from the original. It would be easy to discredit Meurman's original plan in the face of Ervi's revision, but that would be missing the point. While town planning requires a specific physical plan, it also requires reexamination periodically, as new ideas and conditions occur. For although particular conditions can change, like resident or tributary population, the needs of people do not. Principle should guide, and exigencies should be cause for the reappraisal of a particular plan. Planning is a process, but at specific moments the process requires specific physical designs for action.

Tapiola's center was not started until four years after the competition was held. Before work began, however, a second neighborhood was well under way.

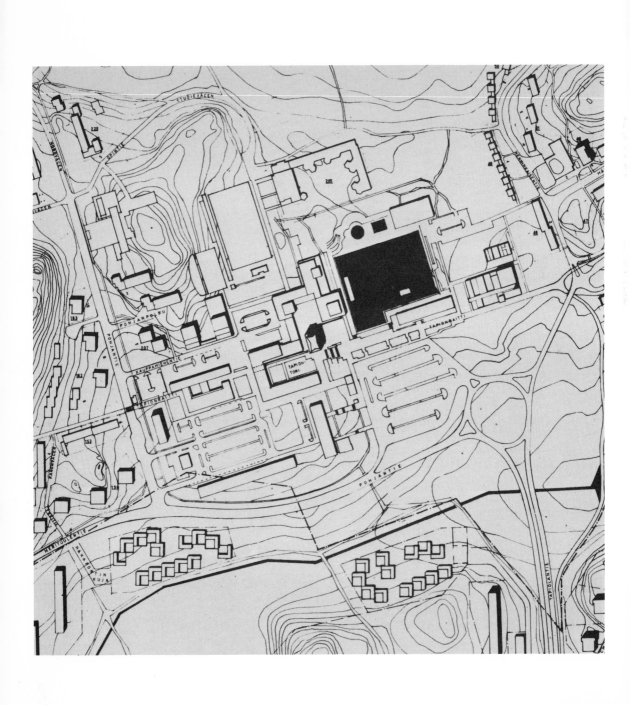

37.
The original concept of the
town center of Tapiola,
proposed by Arne Ervi. The
model view is southwest-
ward. The center would
be dominated by a
fourteen-story office tower
at whose foot would be a
shopping center. To the
right are a theater and
library, then an elementary
school. In the foreground is
a church. To the left is a
hotel. Just above the
parking lot is a central
information pavilion.

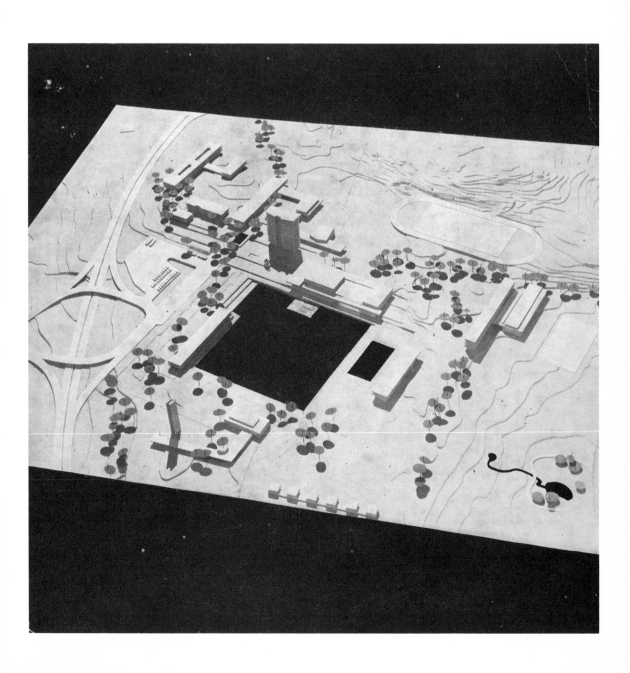

38.
A model of the town center
showing the church, the
proposed hotel in the
foreground, the proposed
theater to the right of the
tower, and the recently
completed Heikintori
department store above and
to the west of the shopping
plaza.

39.
Model of the fourteen-story
tower alongside the pool.
The theater is to the right.
Behind the tower is the
shopping plaza. The
information pavilion (not
shown) is to the left.

Parking

40.
The town center, looking
westward.
41.
The town center at night,
with the tower penthouse
illuminated as a beacon.
The fountain is also
illuminated.

42.
The approach to the town
center on a winter night, at
Christmas season.
43.
The approach to the town
center. The stairs are very
carefully proportioned for an
easy ascent. Their breadth
and elegance establishes a
sense of occasion.

44.
The town center shopping
plaza.
45.
A not-incidental detail.

46.
Along the pool. The small
strip of ground along the
wall enables trees to grow.
The trees cast delicate
shadow patterns on the
wall. The eye is refreshed
by the composition of
intimate and slightly
quivering surfaces,
horizontal and vertical.
47.
The view from the rooftop
cafe. The whole town is
visible, as well as the
Helsinki skyline and the
coastal archipelago.

48.
Looking back on the pool.
The swimming hall is in the
distance.
49.
Looking south to the sea,
view from the top of the
central tower building.

50.
The swimming pool. The
walls open during warm
weather. The tower is seen
to the left.

51.
"Never more than 250 yards from your doorstep to the nearest shops." This map illustrates how this principle has been worked out in the planning of Tapiola. The smallest circles (subcenters) have a radius of 250 yards. As can be seen, these circles cover practically all the inhabited areas of Tapiola. From many places the consumer can reach several centers "within the perambulator distance." The system is completed by village and neighborhood centers with a radius of 330 yards. The biggest circle (the Town Center) shows the maximum walking distance of 380 yards from the Central Tower.

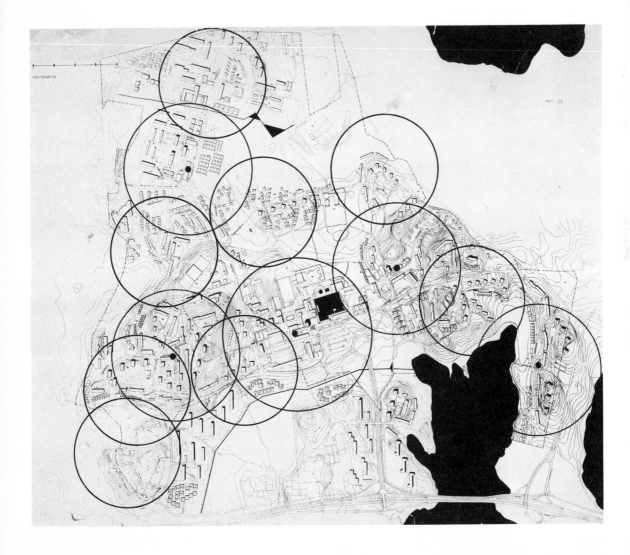

52.
The Heikintori mall with a
fashion show.

53.
The recent extension of the
town center, ''Heikintori.''
This is a department store
with a central enclosed
mall. The view looks
westward. The apartment
towers were designed by
Viljo Revell. They are a
prominent element of the
Tapiola skyline.
54.
The Heikintori mall.

55.
A study model for the
expansion of the town
center. A is the original
shopping plaza. B is the
department store, Heikintori,
and C is the expanded
center, a region-serving
facility.

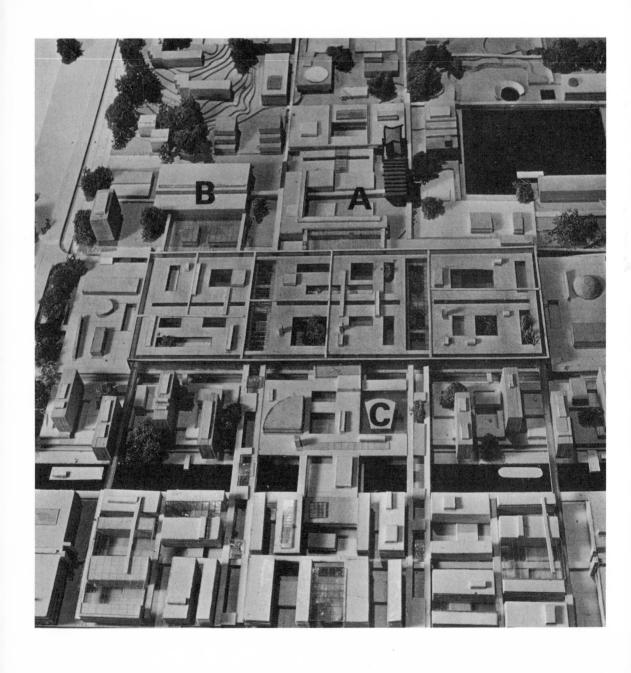

56.
Study plan of the expanded
town center. Note the
position of the pool, upper
right. This center would
have several levels. It would
be served by underpassing
roads (R). A canal (C) is also
a possibility. A further
extension is possible to the
south. Parking is underneath.

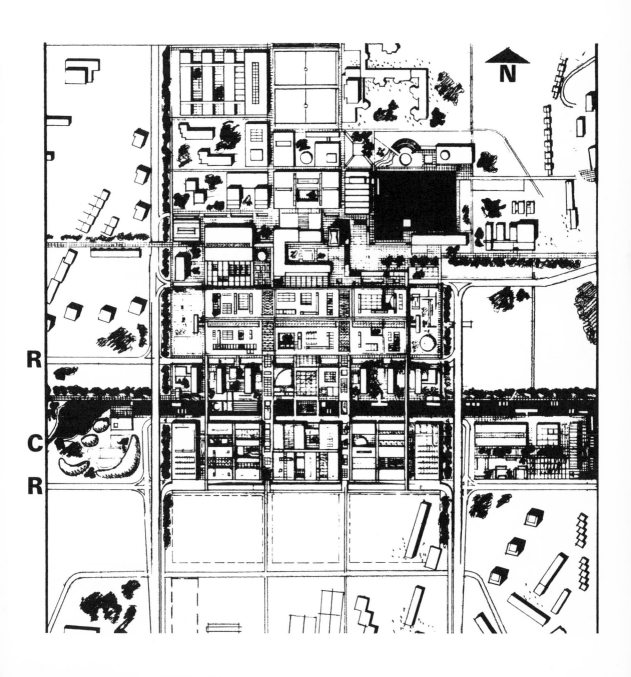

57.
Cross-section study for the
expanded town center,
showing two to three levels
of below-grade parking, a
canal, mass transit stops,
malls, escalators, and a
variety of above-grade uses.
The original town center is
to the right. The section is
looking westward.

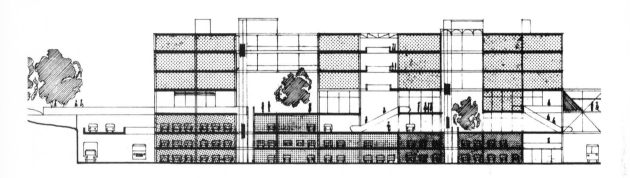

X

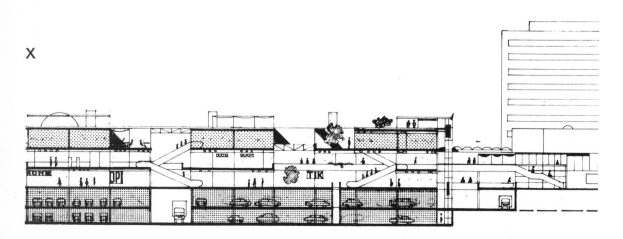

X

X

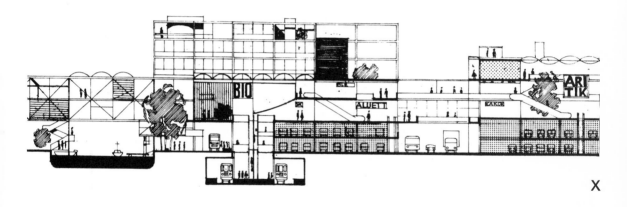

X

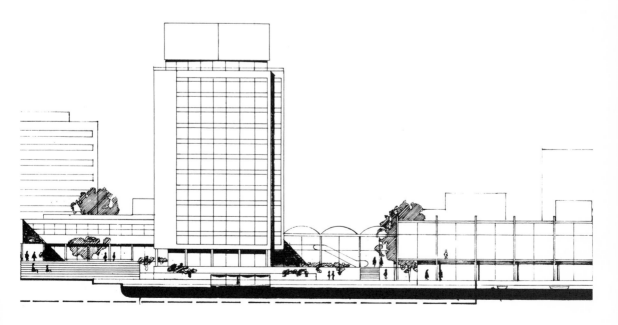

58.
The multilevel concept of
the town center extension.
The lowest level is for
auto access and service.
The second level is for
parking, and the third
is for pedestrians.

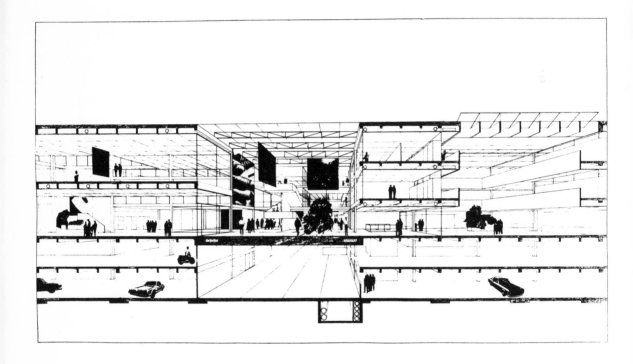

59.
The church in the town
center, designed by Arno
Ruusuvuori.
60.
Model of the high
school in the town center,
designed by Jorma Järvi. It
is on the northern edge of
the center.

The Second or Western Neighborhood In
1955, it was time to begin to develop a site and
building plan for the next building phase, the
second or western neighborhood. The task was
again assigned as a team effort, this time to the
following nine architects: Arne Ervi, Veikko Malmio, Osmo Sipari, Viljo Revell, Heikki Siren,
Jorma Jarvi, Aulis Blomstedt, Markus Tavio, and
L. R. Pinomaa. The first six of these architects
had all competed and placed in the architectural
competition for the town center of Tapiola. On
the basis of topography the western neighborhood was divided into nine subareas. Each of
the nine architects acted both as an architect
and urban designer, and each offered suggestions as to architectural design and site layout.
Veikko Malmio, who had won the second prize
in the town center competition, made the design
for the western neighborhood center and its surrounding residential area. Viljo Revell was responsible for a large housing group on the site's
hilltop. For this he designed a building group
that forms a very important part of the silhouette
of Tapiola.

A most interesting task began when the nine
architects and Asuntosäätiö's planning department attempted to coordinate the nine separate
subneighborhoods. The problem was making
them match, particularly along the edges where
they met. It was a difficult task. More than a
decade later one must admit that the idea itself
was not necessarily bad, but the architects were
too many in number, and the subneighborhoods
assigned to them were too small. Four architects
would have been more workable. But through
such experiences one learns.

Heikki Siren, in the cluster on Iltarusko Street,
and Viljo Revell, on the top of the hill, were
most successful. Veikko Malmio created a neighborhood center totally composed of low buildings. It has an intimate human scale. It differs
considerably from the eastern neighborhood
center, and it has a feeling of warmth and
individuality.

One of Tapiola's planning principles, evident
also in the western neighborhood, is the consis-
tent placement of multistory buildings alternately
with low buildings. Even in new towns this is not
practiced as commonly and intimately as in Tapiola. The general objection to this arrangement
is that single-family housing and multistory
buildings do not mix well. In Tapiola the two
were combined for the purpose of fostering casual social mixture. Low buildings and private
gardens contribute a sense of spaciousness and
variety to high buildings. High buildings, in turn,
furnish population concentrations that make high
levels of public service feasible. Previously,
high-rise buildings enjoyed the advantage of better services and low-rise for spaciousness. Together, however, these two modes of building
benefit each other and make it possible to have
an urban environment with variety, beauty, and
good services.

61.
An air view of part of the
western neighborhood,
looking northwest. The
central power plant is
visible, as well as the roof
of the Weilin & Göös
printing company plant.
62.
Air view of the western
neighborhood in winter,
looking westward from the
center.

63.
The roof structure of the
Weilin & Göös printing
plant. The architect was
Ruusuvuori and the
structural engineer, Bertel
Ekengren.

64.
The work areas of the
Weilin & Göös printing
plant. Each column supports
7,260 square feet of floor
area, as a result of the
unique structural system.

65.
The neighborhood center of
the western neighborhood.

66.
Landscaping in the western
neighborhood center. At
each main point of arrival or
gathering place in Tapiola
the visitor is greeted by
flowers and planting.

67.
Tower apartments in the
western neighborhood,
designed by Viljo Revell.

68.
The western neighborhood
center at a busy hour of the
afternoon.

69.
Town houses designed by
Kaija and Heikki Siren,
1960, in the western
neighborhood.
70.
The Siren row houses. Floor
plans, 970 square feet.
(scale 1:220, or 1″ =
17′ +, approximately)

71.
A portion of the western
neighborhood. The Siren
row houses are on the left.
72.
Apartment plan in the
apartment houses to the
right. Designed by Keija and
Heikki Siren, 1961. 716
square feet. (scale 1:220)

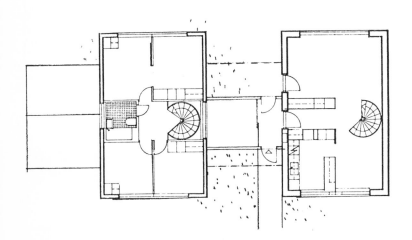
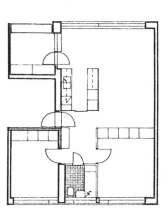

73.
"Chain houses" designed
by Viljo Revell. This was his
last work in Tapiola before
his death.
74.
Site plan of Revell's "chain
house." Note the common
garage, which safeguards
the site from automobile
intrusion, cuts down noise
and road surface, and
allows more greenery.

75.
The common garages for
Revell's "chain houses."
Here is a detail that goes a
long way in preserving the
real assets of a site.
Chatham village in
Pittsburgh used the same
idea.

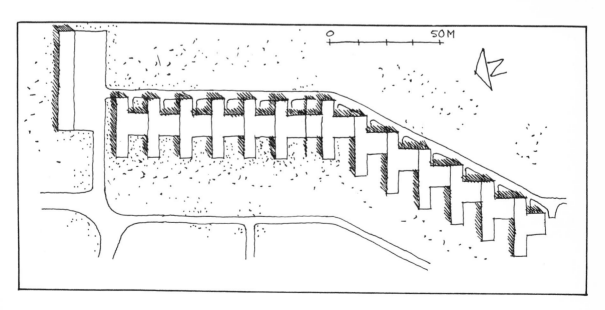

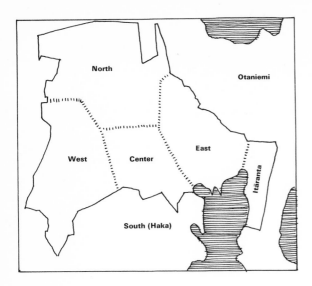

The Third or Northern Neighborhood In 1958, when it was decided to plan the northern neighborhood, an invited competition* was organized among the architects Aarne Ervi, Olli Kivinen, and Pentti Ahola. The winner was Pentti Ahola. Its linear and mathematical severity were in strong contrast with the planning used in both the eastern and western neighborhood. The result was rather interesting. For some time the opinion was voiced, especially among younger architects, that the planning of most of Tapiola was too "romantic." Their view arose from the fact that Tapiola's site planning and building grouping did not follow a rectilinear or geometric pattern, which they felt to be proper. Instead it followed ground contour or stands of trees or rock outcroppings. Hence the label "romantic."

In the north neighborhood it was decided to allow "un-romantic" designers to show what they preferred. The result was a site pattern that followed the geometric layout. Finnish site planning is characterized by a free disposition of buildings according to topography, sunlight, wind, and view, so that some site plans seem disorganized to the casual eye. In fact, this disorder belies a profound basis of order, a basis in natural site conditions. Nevertheless, Ahola's rectilinear layout is skillfully done and poses an interesting contrast to other neighborhoods. It is, in fact, an excellent thing to have neighborhood units of different character. Although the landscaping of the northern neighborhood is not complete, it is possible to compare it with the older

* An architectural competition, in which specific participants are invited to submit proposals, as contrasted with the more familiar "open" competition, which any qualified architect may enter.

neighborhoods. Each has its merits. As it happens, the majority of the thousands of expert visitors who have examined Tapiola regard Tapiola's first neighborhood, the eastern section, as the freshest, most human, and most inspiring part of the town.

In addition to the competitions for the urban center and the neighborhoods, competitions have been staged for groups of buildings such as Suvikumpu, and particular types of buildings, such as the prefabricated town houses of Aarnivalkea. The invited competition for Suvikumpu was won by Reima Pietilä. A terrace house competition was won by Heikki Siren and Puutalo Oy (Timber House Ltd.). A competition for the secondary school of Tapiola was won by Jorma Järvi, and that for Tapiola's church by Aarno Ruusuvuori. He also designed the excellent factory of Weilin & Goos, a printing firm.

In order to take full advantage of Finnish experience in multistoried building, Professor Esko Suhonen, long-time chief of ARAVA's technical department, and K. A. Pinomaa, an architect, were engaged for certain building commissions. Pinomaa brought (in the mid-1950s) the most recent experience and information of HSB, Sweden's largest planning and cooperative building enterprise. Much attention has been given to the question of low-rise housing,* and Asuntosäätiö has commissioned many architects who have displayed skill in designing this type of building. Tapiola has probably a greater collection of different types of houses—row, terrace, and atrium houses; one-, two-, and four-family houses—than anywhere else in Finland. Among the architects

* A common term covering one-family houses, town or row houses, semidetached houses, and courtyard houses.

responsible for these are Heikki and Kaija Siren,
K. A. Pinomaa, Viljo Revell, Aulis Blomstedt,
Aarne Ervi, Pentti Ahola, Veikko Malmio, Jorma
Järvi, Bror Söderman, and Heikki Koskelo. In
short, then, Asuntosäätiö has tried by every
available means to create opportunities for the
best designers in Finland to contribute to the solution of the intricate problems of the dwelling
place of modern man and his family.

  As all these neighborhoods took shape, the picture became one of a town center separated
from its surrounding neighborhoods by open
spaces. Promenades from each neighborhood
lead to the town center, which allows no through
traffic. In addition to the main center, there are
three independent neighborhood centers, serving
approximately 5,000 to 6,000 inhabitants each.
Grocery stores are located within a radius of
about 250 yards, measured from individual
dwellings. Asuntosäätiö thinks of this dimension
as ''perambulator distance.''

76.
Model of the winning
design for the competition
for the upper portion of the
northern neighborhood,
designed by a team led by
Pentti Ahola, 1958. Later
the concept was refined
considerably. The view is to
the northeast. Tapiola center
lies to the lower right.

77.
A later refinement of the
Ahola concept, looking to
the east. The center of
Tapiola lies to the upper
right.

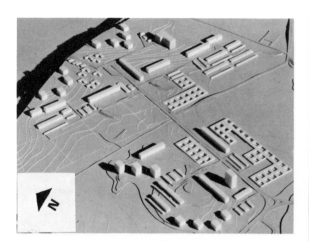

78.
Air view of a portion of the
northern neighborhood
looking eastward. Actually,
the area in the middle
distance is as much a part
of the town center. The
open field to the upper left
is the site of the proposed
"children's town." The
single houses in the
foreground were designed
by Pentti Ahola. Those in
the middle distance were
designed by Jorma Järvi.

Study model for the
children's town. The view
is looking to the northwest.
The locale is the now-empty
area between the eastern and
the northern neighborhoods.

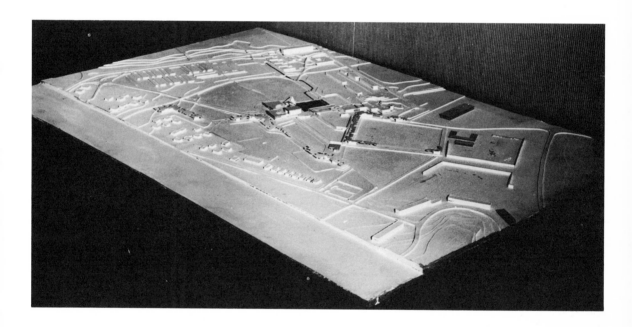

80.
Single-family house
designed by Pentti Ahola,
1957. Four bedrooms,
kitchen, dining area, living
room, bath-laundry-sauna,
and storage room. 1070
square feet. (scale 1:220+)

81.
Single-family house
designed by Jorma Järvi,
1957. Three bedrooms,
living-dining room, kitchen,
bath, sauna, storage. 870
square feet. (scale 1:220+)

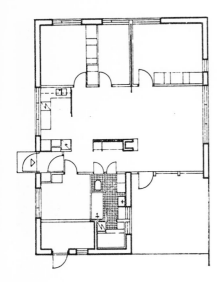

82.
Model of the small single
houses north of the town
center, designed by Jorma
Järvi.

83.
Gardens of the single
homes designed by Jorma
Järvi.

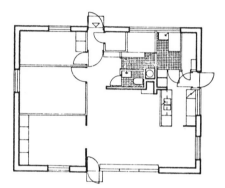

84.
A shop in the northern
neighborhood. The
generous porch is a shelter
for baby carriages and an
after-school meeting place
for schoolchildren.

85.
''H'' houses designed by
Veikko Malmio.
86.
The ''H'' houses in winter.

87.
A group of detached row
houses designed by Heikki
Koskelo, 1965–1966.
Fourteen houses comprise
the group. They share a
swimming pool, near which
is a common parking
garage.
88a.
The detached houses
designed by Heikki Koskelo
and the planning
department of Asuntosäätiö.

88b.
The swimming pool of the
fourteen-house
group.

88c.
Plan of the
fourteen-house
group.

The Northern Neighborhood 142-143

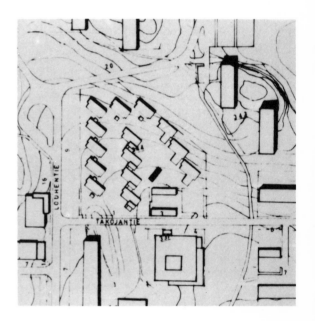

89.
Two-story town houses in the
northern neighborhood,
designed by Heikki Siren.
Note the illuminated house
number. It is standard
throughout Tapiola.

90.
The "Arab village" row
houses designed by Veikko
Malmio.

91.
A four-story walk-up
apartment house in the
northern neighborhood.

92.
Two-bedroom apartment
designed by Viljo Revell,
1958. Note the large
storage closet. 700 square
feet. (scale 1:220)

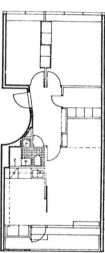

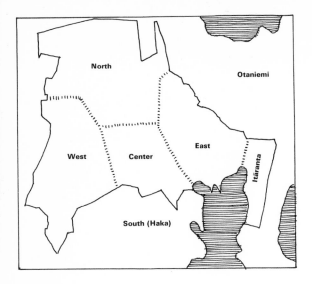

Itäranta An additional area adjoining the original eastern neighborhood was bought by Asuntosäätiö five years after the main part of the Hagalund estate was purchased in 1951. It was called Itäranta. The seller was once again Dr. Arne Grahn. Asuntosäätiö had attempted to procure this area in connection with the first purchase, but Dr. Grahn would not agree until five years later. For this reason, the planning of this area was not started before 1957. This time the planning department of Asuntosäätiö was responsible for the entire plan. The area in question is rather small (a little more than 65 acres), but it is beautifully situated on the shore of Otsolahti Bay, a tiny inlet of the Gulf of Finland. Before planning started, the site's topography and character were carefully studied. It was decided to create a common green space proceeding from the water and extending all around Otsolahti Bay. The dwellings are located on different levels, so that almost every dwelling has a view of the Bay. The first row, closest to the common green, is composed of low one-family houses of bungalow type. In the second row are either two-story row houses or three-story walk-ups. On the top of the hill seven-story high-rise houses are located. Parking facilities and central garages are concentrated at only three points. Only one-family houses and row houses have private garages. When the site design of this area was completed, it was necessary to select architects. For the multistory housing projects it was decided to use only three architects. Alvar Aalto agreed to design the high-rise buildings on the top of the ridge. The design of the remaining apartment houses was assigned to Aarne Ervi and Heikki Siren. The choice of the architects for the low-

rise housing was less critical, but the planning had to be approved by the planning department of Asuntosäätiö.

There are only two streets in the whole residential area, one of them paralleling the shore—well away from the shore—and the other running along the ridge of the isthmus. Both streets are cul-de-sacs. At the center of the area is located an intimate patio, around which is placed a shopping subcenter to serve a population of about 2,000. Once again the principle ''no more than 250 yards from your doorstep to the shopping center'' was followed. A staircase from the patio leads to a supervised playground. Incidentally, these are called ''aunty parks,'' after the custom of Finnish children of referring to their nursemaids as ''aunty.'' The pedestrian way, starting from the subcenter, leads from the playground toward the water edge, follows the seashore of Otsolahti Bay, passes the Marina, and ends in the town center of Tapiola.

The Itäranta residential area includes a group of four connected houses, all in one story. This particular group is of masonry, specifically, light buff tiles with oiled teak trim. The trim gives a beautiful dark brown tone. All are set against tall trees and run parallel to the shore of Otsolahti Bay, from which they are set back about 40 yards. There are several remarkable things about this group. To the observer they appear quite obviously to have been the work of a single architect. The four houses are connected, having exactly the same materials, scale, and cornice design. Their floor plans, however, are entirely different. Most remarkably, they are the work of three different architects who agreed to use the same materials and construction motif—Arne

Ervi, Heikki Koskelo, and Markus Tavio. Their design as a group is testimony to some of the outstanding characteristics of Finnish architecture: using a limited palette of materials, letting nature dominate, playing horizontal architectural masses against the verticals of the trees and the up and down of the site profile, and solving simple problems in a simple and direct way. This group, too, testifies to the importance of carefully and deeply thought-out site planning.

At the same time, it is a rule in Tapiola that the shoreline belongs to everyone. Thus it is possible for an occupant of one of the four houses to see a passerby strolling across the edge of his own land. Apparently this is not a problem, since it happens so infrequently, due very likely to the overall density of Tapiola, coupled with the careful disposition of open space.

Itäranta has a particularly interesting urban design feature concerning Tapiola's silhouette. Every town should have visual coherence and identity. All great cities have a visible image that expresses their personality. Tapiola has the advantage of being approached across an open body of water, an inlet that separates it from Helsinki. Thus there was the opportunity to present Tapiola in silhouette to arriving residents and visitors. The silhouette of Tapiola is dominated by the 13-story office tower, whose top is illuminated as a solid panel of light about two stories high. At night it becomes a beacon. In addition, four tower residences in the western neighborhood, designed by Viljo Revell, further reinforce the silhouette. The respect for silhouette is also shown by Aalvar Aalto's response when he was asked to design seven tall buildings in Itäranta. At first he was quite reluctant to do so because of the change they would effect on Tapiola's skyline. Later he consented, when he was sure that his additions would not obtrude.

Aalto's design is most interesting and subtle. The buildings are fan-shaped in plan, but simple blocklike masses in profile. Thus, from afar, they are visually passive. Although they are prominent in Tapiola's overall silhouette, they do not disturb it. On the other hand, seen close up, the buildings have a very dynamic skyline silhouette because of the fanlike facades. It is as if the building changed its shape for different viewing conditions, when in fact it is simply the observer who has changed his point of view.

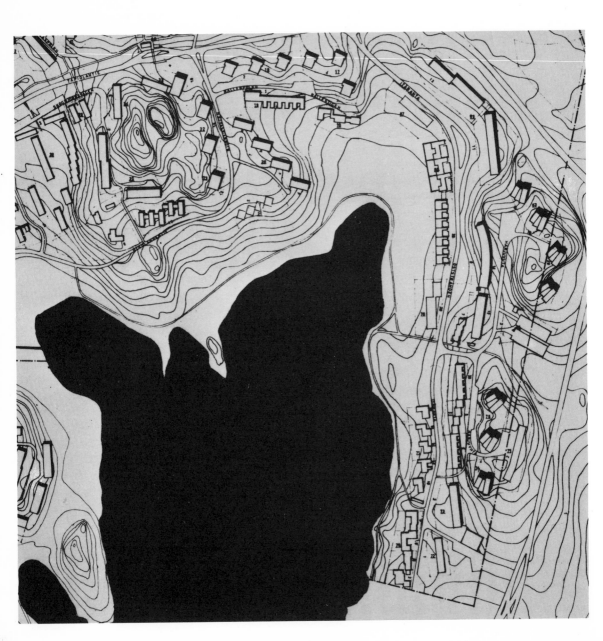

93.
Site plan of the group of
four one-family houses in
Itäranta, designed by three
different architects for four
different clients, yet all
employing the same building
materials, scale, cornice,
design, and character.
The architects were Ervi,
Koskelo, and Tavio.

94.
The group of four single-
family houses in Itäranta.

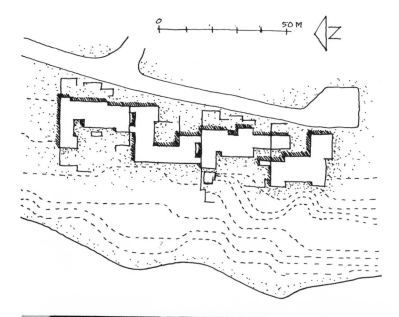

95.
An "aunty park," with
"aunty" in attendance. The
little houses and fences
were designed by a stage
designer and built by an old
carpenter. They resemble
traditional wooden Finnish
houses in form.

96.
A wading pond in Itäranta.

97.
A walk-up apartment
building in Itäranta,
designed by Ervi and Siren.
High density was achieved
without sacrifice of livability.

98.
Plan of row houses in
Itäranta, designed by Bror
Söderman. The houses are
on a slope. Entry is on the
upper level. The lower level
has a sauna and several
storage rooms.
99.
Row houses designed by
Bror Söderman, a staff
architect of Asuntosäätiö.

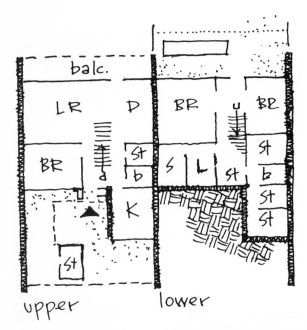

upper   lower

100.
Model of apartment houses
in Itäranta designed by
Alvar Aalto. From afar the
building masses are very
neutral, the tops being flat
and the height to width
nearly forming a square in
silhouette.
101.
High-rise apartments in
Itäranta designed by
Alvar Aalto.

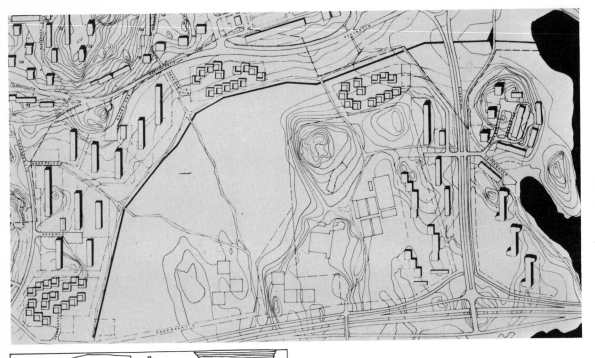

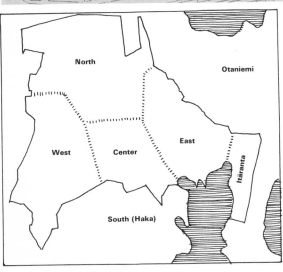

102.
The southern
neighborhood was
built by HAKA. It
includes medium-rise
slab apartments (below)
and the atrium houses
(next page).

103.
Plan of the patio houses in
the southern neighborhood.
Pentti Ahola, architect.
MBr —Master bedroom
Br —Bedroom
B   —Bath
K   —Kitchen
D   —Dining
LR —Living room
Sy —Study
S   —Sauna
St —Storage
UH —Utility, hobby

104.
Patio house in the southern
neighborhood.
105.
Site plan of the Ahola patio
houses in the southern
neighborhood.

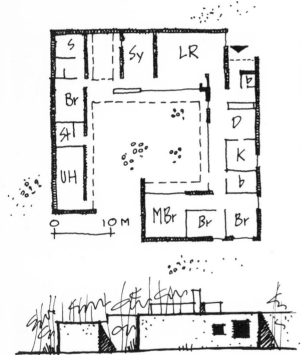

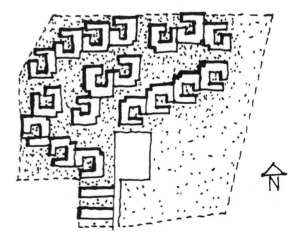

106.
Courtyard of Ahola's group
of patio houses in the
southern neighborhood.

The Southern Neighborhood 156-157

Tapiola Overall Tapiola's development follows a sequence that started in 1952 and will conclude by about 1970:

1. The eastern neighborhood, 1952–1956; 5,000 residents.
2. The western neighborhood, 1957–1960; 5,000 residents.
3. The town center, 1958–1961–1970–to ultimate completion.
4. The northern neighborhood, 1958–1967; 5,000 residents.
5. The southern neighborhood, 1961–1965; 3,000 residents.
6. The Itäranta portion of the eastern neighborhood, 1958–1964; 2,000 residents.
7. The children's town, 1969—.

At this writing, two main efforts remain before Tapiola is completed. The town center is to be expanded and greater auto parking space provided. Second, a children's ''amusement town'' is being planned for part of the open space between the eastern and northern neighborhoods. The children's town will be an area devoted to children's play. Naturally, Tapiola abounds in play spaces for children of all ages, from sandboxes to soccer fields, but the children's town will be in effect a Tivoli of juvenile amusements.

Tapiola's expanded town center will be full of action at all times. The objective is to make it into a shopping district with as much variety as Helsinki's main shopping thoroughfare, Alexander Street. In addition, there will be hotels, office and administrative buildings, and some apartments. The apartments will be along the outer edge bordering the green spaces. The center is conceived as a series of levels with parking underneath. The upper pedestrian level is conceived as a series of plazas and covered shopping streets, linked to the existing plaza in the present town center. Through traffic from the east and west goes underground.

According to the plans the center will be extended toward the south. No final decisions have yet been made, but it seems obvious that the extension will be realized in two or more phases. In the first phase the original town center, designed by architect Aarne Ervi, will be extended to the main highway leading from Helsinki westward. In the next phase, possibly in the 1980s, it will reach the seashore, so giving the town center a direct connection with the Gulf of Finland and the lovely archipelago. The future squares and patios will grow up from the sea surrounded by beautifully located marinas. At that time Tapiola will be a township of 80,000 inhabitants.

As for Tapiola's land-use composition, 54.2 percent is open green space, with 24.2 percent for housing. The residential land area is half row and single family (77.3 acres or 31.3 hectares) and half multistory (84.3 acres or 34.1 hectares). Public buildings occupy 5.1 percent of the land, industrial buildings 3.7 percent, and commercial buildings 2.3 percent. Land for all forms of circulation—streets, paths, and parking—occupies only 9.5 percent of the total. Tapiola's land-use composition is as follows:

Portion	Acres	Hectares	%
Housing	161.6	65.4	24.2
Public Buildings	34.0	13.8	5.1
Commericial Buildings	13.8	5.6	2.3
Industrial Buildings	24.7	10.0	3.7
Garages	7.2	2.9	1.0
Common Green and Parks	362.0	146.5	54.2
Traffic Areas	63.7	25.8	9.5
Total	667.0	270.0	100.0

The housing site areas are as follows:

	Acres	Hectares	%
Single Family	25.7	10.4	15.9
Row	51.6	20.9	32.0
Multistory	84.3	34.1	52.1
Total	161.6	65.4	100.0

During the initial stages of planning, it was decided as a matter of policy to establish as many jobs as possible for residents either in the town or close by. Therefore, certain zones, separated from the residential units by green belts, were reserved for small-scale light industries. The site of Tapiola's small industries lies between the western and northern neighborhood units. In addition to the central heating plant located in this area, numerous enterprises and small-scale industries are accommodated in the small industry building, completed in 1960. The most impressive building, however, is the Weilin & Göös printshop with its interesting hanging roof construction. (In the printing room there is only one vertical support for every 729 square meters.) Only a wall of glass separates the modern printing presses from untouched nature; architecture and nature are blended flawlessly together. When totally completed, this enterprise by itself provides employment for 700 workers.

Selection of the industries and enterprises that are allowed in Tapiola is guided by a simple rule: the industries must not produce soot, smoke, or noise. In other words the industries of Tapiola must not disturb the residents. As a result the industries operate for the most part on electric power.

Another aspect of planning concerns parks and play spaces. Experienced municipal authorities smiled when in 1952 Asuntosäätiö described its plans for abundant landscaping for parks, lawns, and large flower beds. More than one-third of the population would be comprised of infants and children, and the authorities warned that, after the children had occupied the town for a short while, not a single growing thing would remain. This has not been the case. The lawns are green and the flower beds full and quite undamaged. Asuntosäätiö concluded that children who grow up in an open and happy environment do not regard nature as an enemy but as a friend. It is also likely that in the view of authorities city children seem to be destructive of plants and greenery because those are among the few things in their environment that they can manipulate with their hands. Children must touch things, move things, and change things in order to learn and grow. For city children who have limited play space and even more limited greenery, plants and trees appear as objects of destruction to the undiscerning eyes of authority. Where they are plentiful, what seems to be vandalism ceases to be a problem. On the subject of vandalism, neither the state nor the municipality has hired a single policeman. There is only one policeman in Tapiola, but he was hired by the housing companies and serves mainly as a leader of youth groups. With this degree of know-how, and by demonstrating commitment to its stated ideals, Asuntosäätiö began to prove its point.

Of great importance to designers and administrators was Asuntosäätiö's range of approaches in procuring designs. In fact it has taken five different approaches on different occasions. First is the use of design teams, as in the east neighborhood. Second is the open competition, as in the town center. Third is the subdivision of a site into succinct design pieces, each piece assigned to an architect, some of these architects being selected from the previous open competition. This is how the western neighborhood was designed. Fourth is the invited competition, as in the northern neighborhood. Fifth is urban design done by staff planners and architects, as in Itäranta.

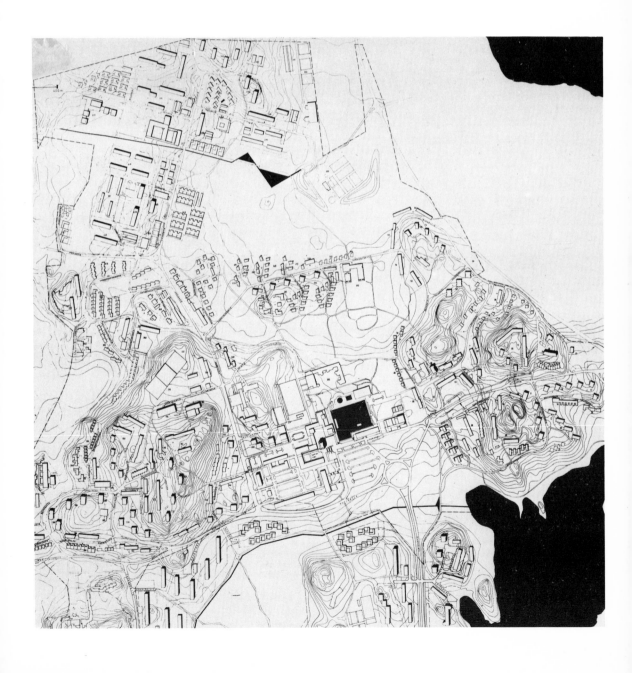

108.
Component portions of
Tapiola.

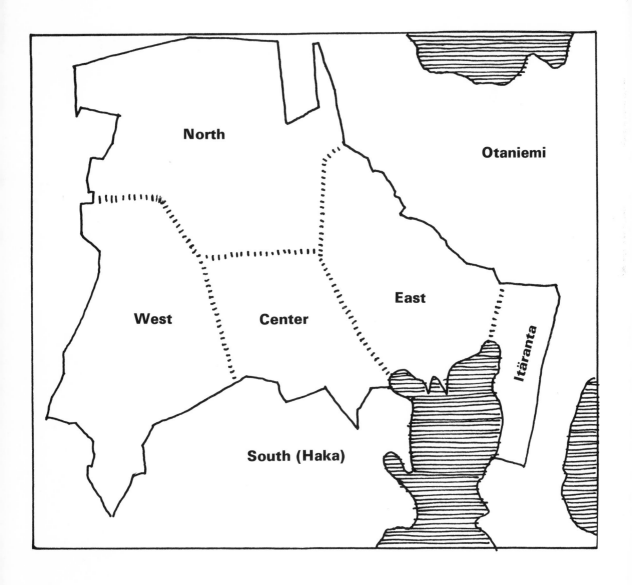

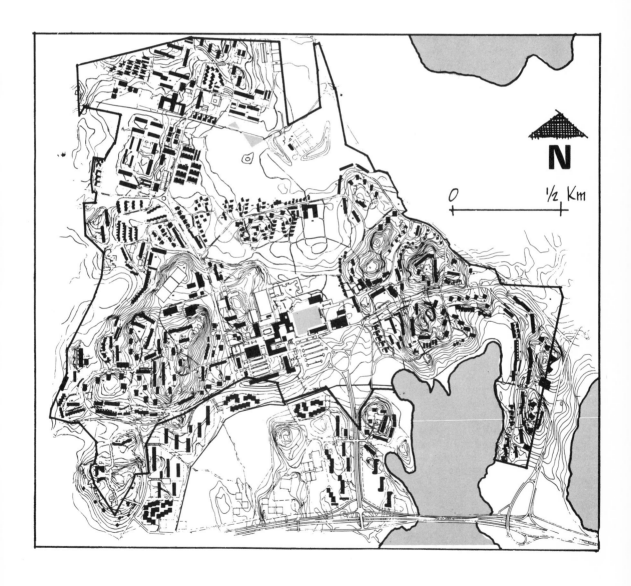

Administration and Operation

Asuntosäätiö sets policy through a council of sixteen members, six being nominated by each of the six member organizations. The remaining nine members are technical specialists, such as economists, engineers, architects, and so forth, who complement the politicians. The council elects a board of nine who meet weekly. The board has "standing" members and "supplementary" members, the "standing" members representing the constituent organizations. Working operations are handled by three departments: planning, technical, and administrative, and the division of tasks is quite clear. The planning department plans everything from the town plan to dwellings and public buildings. The planning department is also responsible for designing the landscaping, gardening, and even such details as kiosks, street lighting, advertising signs, and decorative illumination. The technical department builds what the planning department plans. Finally, the administrative department makes life pulsate in the town. All deputies or assistants are always present at meetings to obtain information firsthand. Every Tuesday there is a meeting of the managing directors (planning, technical, and administrative).

In the course of its experience Asuntosäätiö learned conclusively that decisive control power over the land, ownership if possible, is one of the most important conditions for rational planning. Asuntosäätiö also learned that plans must be realized fairly rapidly, for plans become obsolete quickly, and their cost becomes a loss. It learned the importance of firm discipline and control over all operations during the building period so that plans would not be spoiled.

Asuntosäätiö saw that it had to guard against expedient alterations that were demanded daily, alterations that compromise the plan unnecessarily. It saw the fallacy of thinking that the job ends with the drawing of the master plan or a town plan—that is where the work begins. At most, only a quarter of the work is done after the plans are drawn; the most difficult problems are yet to be encountered.

Further, all that has been planned must be made to live and breathe. A community must be transformed from roads and buildings into a living organism of the people who constitute societies. The hearts of those societies must be made to beat. The organization that plans and builds a community must know how to bring this about. In short, Asuntosäätiö found that modern community planning is dynamic, creative work that can only succeed with firm management and inspired leadership.

Asuntosäätiö was set up to pursue broad purposes without seeking direct financial profit. Its aims were to try to overcome the housing shortage, raise general housing standards, develop communities, and make integrated towns according to modern planning concepts. To realize its ideals and to create the conditions for building entire areas, Asuntosäätiö has the power, under paragraph three of its articles of constitution, to acquire necessary land, take steps to produce appropriate master plans or construction plans, or to have alterations made in these plans under its own supervision and in accord with a general plan. If necessary, Asuntosäätiö can assume all the tasks for promoting the realization of its building areas, such as the actual construc-

tion of houses, public buildings, sports and recreational areas, streets, roads, sewers, and water
mains. A special paragraph empowers it to pursue research and publishing activity in housing
policy.

However, Asuntosäätiö sees the translation of
these tasks as far more than the production of
streets and buildings. A town is people as well
as streets and buildings, people who are basically private individuals but must also act as responsible participating citizens, not just tenants.
To establish a genuine community spirit right at
the start, then, was one of Asuntosäätiö's aims.

Tapiola as a Cross-Section Community As already stressed, the aim of the Tapiola project
from the outset was the construction of a whole
town, a community. It was not intended to follow the practice of house-by-house construction
or to create isolated residential areas in a patch-
work pattern. The reason for this is quite simple.
It is possible to achieve, at most, only 25 percent of the basic needs of people inside their
dwellings; the remaining 75 percent must be
satisfied outside their houses. When a resident
moves to a new address, he asks, "Where are
the children's playgrounds, the kindergartens,
the nurseries? Where can the young have free
scope for their activities? Where can they let off
their excess energy? Where are the schools, not
only the elementary schools but also the voca-
tional, secondary, and high schools? Where do
I do my shopping? What services does this local-
ity offer? What leisure-time and cultural activities
are available? Where do we satisfy our need for
social contact with other people when we want
and need it?"

Today's urban dweller desires all of this. However, it was the view of Asuntosäätiö that he is
unwilling to realize these desires without regard
to other negative factors. To have all his needs
satisfied, he is no longer willing to breathe polluted air, to put up with the din of traffic noise
or with foul-smelling shorelines, or to let his children play in backyards and gutters. Today's ur-
banite does not want to be lost in the crowd, jos-
tled and wearied at overcrowded shops, or left
to talk to himself at self-service shops where
there is no social contact. The target set by
Asuntosäätiö was that Tapiola was to be a totally
functioning community. To do this, it should first
achieve as much independence as possible in its
services and working places. And, second, it
should have a full-size urban center. A variety of
services have, in fact, quickly developed in the
area, often earlier than the number of inhabitants would suggest. The final number of dwelling units in "Tapiola proper" will be 4,575. In
discussing this matter at an international congress,* Professor Leo Aario, of the University of
Helsinki's Department of Geography, made the
following comments:

In Tapiola there are at present over 3,000
working places, that is, for nearly half of the economically active population. About 40% of these
are in industry, 20% in trade, 35% in service
occupations, and 5% in transportation. According to reservations already made, the number of
the working places will nearly double in about
five years. The on-site jobs will then occupy
about 80% of the resident wage earners. This is
a very good result, when we consider that the
occupations of many of the inhabitants cannot

* Lecture held at the 21st International Geographical Congress, Symposium of Urban Geography, Benares, India, November 1968.

be located in Tapiola. These include jobs at the universities, state and provincial administration, etc.

Almost all the people moving to Tapiola already had a job in Helsinki or its vicinity. Thus, the need for local working places was small, and in the beginning their proportion to the economically active population was low: 1959, 20%; 1963, 23%; 1965, 35%; 1968, 50%. The proportion is rapidly increasing and, as mentioned, it will probably be about 80% in 1973.

The present percentage, 50%, does not mean that as many of Tapiola's wage earners need to have their jobs in Tapiola. Half of the jobs are filled by people from the surroundings, even from Helsinki. Most of the present inhabitants have not left their former jobs, but the outside workers found in Tapiola are not able to find accommodation in Tapiola proper because the dwelling house construction program is already completed, and few dwellings have become vacant. With time the working places, however, will be more and more occupied by the local inhabitants. From the standpoint of planning it is sufficient that the planned area has as many working places as wage earners. In the near future, when plans for increasing the number of jobs are realized, Tapiola will fill this requirement.

Many different things have been done to make Tapiola as much of a town for everyone as is possible. It has been already mentioned that 80 percent of the dwelling sites were given over for ARAVA production. That was at a time when some neighboring areas did not offer a single site for this purpose. Another factor was that applicants for residence in Tapiola were five to ten times more than could be accepted. Tenant screening was mainly done by the dwelling allocation committee, which was appointed by the board of Asuntosäätiö. The member organizations, especially SAK (Confederation of Finnish Trade Unions), the Central Association of Ten-

ants, and the Union of Civil Servants, were represented on this committee. The deciding factors in making the selection were need and distribution of social classes. All decisions were submitted to ARAVA for approval.

The key factor was the "saving-for-housing" program begun in the late 1950s. This made it possible for a citizen with a fairly modest income to obtain a dwelling of his own by saving for three to four years. He built his basic deposit in this way. Almost the entire northern neighborhood of Tapiola was constructed through the "saving-for-housing" program, with very good results. A report on Tapiola's dwelling costs (1965) contains a few examples of the lists of residents in some "saving-for-housing" buildings. These give a clear picture of their occupations, income levels, and social standing.

Such are some of the methods used by Asuntosäätiö to create a cross-section community. It is clear that this, like all human activities, has only partly succeeded. There is no such thing as a hundred-percent success in human life. To make it possible to give a more objective picture, we should turn once again to the remarks of Professor Leo Aario.[*]

As there was a multiple number of subscribers for dwelling shares, the shareholders were chosen chiefly by considering the number of the children and the housing conditions of the subscriber at that time. Families with many children and poor housing conditions were privileged. The ARAVA houses have some restrictions concerning size, and their standard is regulated, being neither too high or too low. The maximum size was 1076 square feet (100 square meters), the average being not more than about 612 square feet (57 square meters). Thus the

[*] Ibid.

number of small dwelling units became rather large. This increased the chances of people of modest means, but it did not satisfy people with a higher level of requirements. There was a smaller amount of building lots for them, but at a higher price. Also, they had to furnish the capital themselves. So the population of Tapiola consists of all social classes, from a former prime minister to an office cleaner. A university professor and a janitor live side by side in the same building. Only the size of the flats is different. The cross-section proportion of the social classes are reflected in the election results. In the last parliamentary election 45% of the inhabitants voted for the left parties, which is quite close to the average result over the whole country.

Thus, it seems that the original aim of having all social classes in balanced proportion in Tapiola should have been achieved. However, tax rolls show that taxable income in Tapiola has been notably higher than in surrounding areas, even Helsinki. Thus, the proportion of people with the lowest income is still below average. The reason is not difficult to find. Only 10% of the dwelling houses consist of rental units, and the majority of them belong to industrial establishments which rent apartments to their workers. These represent skilled labor for the most part. Many of them own flats or one-family houses. Too few dwelling units are within the reach of unskilled labor with low incomes. The aim of having an average proportion of all social classes is thus not entirely realized even in Tapiola.

Were a community like Tapiola to become public some low income people would still be left out, which means the formation of a slum elsewhere. To prevent this, a greater number of rented quarters is necessary. As there is hardly enough private capital for this purpose, the building of low-income rental housing should be done by the communities. The renting of flats should go to pay the costs. In order to keep rents low enough, it would probably be necessary to reduce the quality of the dwelling units

somewhat. In every case, however, the residents should have the same attractive surroundings and the same services as more well-to-do people. Thus, even these social groups could be incorporated into a community like Tapiola without changing its character. Very many such houses would hardly be necessary, because the proportion of unskilled labor is diminishing.

Sales and Marketing Asuntosäätiö's method for selling houses is of interest. As the house is bought and built, payment usually goes to the builder in three one-third payments, each of the three sources of funds contributing their proportional share. The first payment is made when the owner signs his contract of purchase; the second third is paid when the house is half built; and the last third is paid when the house is finished. Should the buyer change his mind after making his deposit, his money is returned, minus a small charge. However, this seldom happened because demand was five times as great as supply, and Asuntosäätiö used a carefully tailored system for matching home buyers to the houses they needed. This worked as follows: the first step was to provide a variety of houses for a buyer to choose from. Once he has chosen, he may want some alterations in the model selected. The three categories of changes are these:
1. Small alterations, such as relocation of electric outlets, which are allowed at no cost if request is received in writing prior to a specified date.
2. Medium alterations, such as relocating a door or partition, which are accepted if received in writing prior to a certain date. The buyer must pay ahead of time, however, thus preventing indulgence in foolishness or capricious second thoughts.

3. Major alterations, like adding or subtracting a room, or a major structural alteration, which are not allowed. If a buyer asks for these changes, he has selected the wrong house and is advised to look at the many other models Asuntosäätiö has to offer.

The predominant type of building is the three- to four-story walk-up, which has proved most suitable for Tapiola's gently rolling topography. In addition, there are three- to four-story apartment houses and some tower houses containing small apartments. Several types of terrace houses and semidetached houses have been tried, in both wood and masonry. Most of the houses are of conventional construction, but prefabricated ("component") houses were also built.

Much attention was given to details of interior finish. All kitchens are electric and their fixtures carefully designed, usually standardized. Some dwellings have a bar kitchen. All apartments have a bathroom, but a few single-room units are fitted with a shower instead of a tub. Considerable cupboard space is provided, and every apartment has a space for a refrigerator.

Single-family houses are of several types, ranging from prefabricated wooden houses and one-and-a-half story houses to single-story cellarless masonry bungalows, built on a slab foundation. Asuntosäätiö sought to build dwellings as large as legally permissible. The most appropriate types of family dwellings were found to be single-family houses (five rooms and kitchen, bathroom, and sauna—1,075 square feet) and semidetached houses (four or five rooms, kitchen and bathroom—935 square feet). The multistory blocks intended for families were usually limited to three or four stories and contain walk-up apartments. The most common apartment sizes were (1) four rooms totaling 935 square feet; (2) three rooms totaling 625 to 775 square feet; and (3) two rooms totaling 500 to 600 square feet. Relatively few high buildings have been built. The one- and two-room apartments were intended primarily for childless couples and single persons. The single-room apartments, fully equipped, range in floor area from 260 to 365 square feet.

The best policy is for Asuntosäätiö to build according to the best thinking and to sell to buyers who want what is built. However, Asuntosäätiö has been striving to get somewhat closer to the American system, giving the buyer himself more of a role in decisions.

An interesting insight into Asuntosäätiö's approach is revealed in a policy affecting the two top floors of the central office tower. Those floors are obviously prestigious, being quite prominent and affording fine views in all directions. These two stories should be gathering places for Tapiola's residents, day and night. They should be a vantage point from which the whole town could be seen and a place where the residents would meet in leisure, the town at their feet. This would help to reinforce the sense of community. It was decided that the top floor should be a cafe and the floor just below it a first-class restaurant. To further ensure that it will always remain so and not be shifted to some nonpublic use, Asuntosäätiö retains ownership of these two floors and leases them to a cafe and restaurant operator. They have come to be favorite meeting places, completely casual and unforced, as genuine urban meeting places must

be. As important a meeting place, particularly for young people, is the swimming hall at the northeast corner of the reflecting pool. Its glass walls are opened during periods of warm weather.

Public Information and Assimilation It is not possible to build a beautiful city and automatically expect that only "nice" people will be living there. When trying to create a cross-section community, where all quarters of life and social structure are to be represented, it is necessary to combine town planning with first-class educational and public information activity. An additional remark from the educational and public relations point of view must be made. It is this: everyone's next-door neighbor is very important to him, but not because of his income level. What is really important is his cultural level, habits, manners. That is why it is necessary to take into account public information and education in all phases of urban renewal and new towns activities. There can be no good new towns or good new housing areas without high quality public information and education programs from the very first day.

In Tapiola Garden City these problems were tackled in many different ways. A weekly newspaper called *Tapiola Tänään* (Tapiola Today) is published and distributed free of charge to every household in Tapiola each Thursday. Through this newspaper we are in continuous contact with every resident of Tapiola, acquainting them with one another. We help people with common interests but of different social classes to meet one another through these common interests, which breaks down barriers of all kinds. We

have started clubs for bridge, foreign languages, fishing, motoring, modeling, ceramics, theater activity, and so forth. We have in Tapiola one of the most active youth theater groups in Finland. Here young people not only act and produce but also write their own plays. Some of these plays are the most interesting plays that have been seen in Tapiola so far.

There are three ways that a resident of Tapiola can propose an idea or challenge a decision of Asuntosäätiö:
1. A personal call to the director; this is frequently done.
2. A letter to the editor of the town's newspaper.
3. A sharehold in a housing company (of which all residents are members) can insist that the company's board challenge an action or decision.

Incidentally, the name Tapiola was obtained through a competition. In 1956, a public invitation was extended to name the town. A prize was offered, and four thousand entries produced about one thousand names. Twelve suggested "Tapiola," which means, as mentioned before, "the realm of the kingdom of the woods." Tapiola also happens to be the name of one of Sibelius's best symphonic poems; so, in a sense, the town also has its own symphonic poem.

Another problem for management was assimilation. Tapiola, created as it was from the ground up, had no existing population to aid the process of assimilation. The inhabitants came from many different walks of life. Therefore, Asuntosäätiö anticipated possible difficulties of adjustment.

Asuntosäätiö acknowledged that there were three methods of integrating people of different standards of living: creating an environment for the highest standard of living, for the lowest standard of living, or for something in between. From the outset, Asuntosäätiö's aim was to make a high standard of environment for all people, those in the low-income category as well as those in the highest. In this Asuntosäätiö succeeded, and it was most gratifying to see how quickly the lowest groups adapted to the highest standards. Rightly taken, and with the right help, the opportunity to move is also an opportunity to raise one's standard of living.

At present, about 55 percent of the inhabitants of Tapiola are "white collar" and 45 percent "blue collar." More explicitly, population composition in Tapiola is 24 percent professional, 34 percent managerial, and 42 percent skilled labor. Foreign visitors find it hard to believe that so many people with low and middle incomes live in Tapiola and that this has had practically no negative influence on the appearance, cleanliness, level of culture, or spirit of the community.

Service Companies Approximately 90 percent of Tapiola's dwellings are owned by their occupants. A joint-stock "housing company" is formed for groups of buildings of suitable size before construction is started. Finland has special legislation concerning such companies. The company owns the buildings composing a group, and the resident owns a certain number of shares entitling him to hold a specified flat or dwelling unit. The company is managed by a board that is appointed by the occupants at an annual company meeting.

All joint-stock housing companies in Tapiola are stockholders in the so-called "supply companies," either in Otsolahden Lämpö Oy (for the eastern neighborhood unit) or in Tapiolan Lämpö Oy (for the rest of the town). The supply companies, in turn, own the heating plant, certain business premises and buildings, central garages, and a building in which the present cinema is located. These companies produce the necessary heat and hot water for all housing companies in Tapiola. In addition, the supply companies are responsible for the house manager's offices as well as for certain supply and service duties. In Tapiola there are four house manager's offices that are responsible for the bookkeeping of all the housing companies. The house manager's offices also collect rents and other payments for the housing companies, and they also pay bills that become due. The cost of the house manager's offices is shared by all the housing companies. Thus, the total cost per housing company can be kept to a minimum. The supply companies of Tapiola derive their income from the housing companies in the form of heating tariffs, house manager's tariffs, and so forth. Additional income for the supply companies is derived from the rents paid by the occupants of the business premises that the companies own and rent. A part of the common income of the supply companies is used to pay certain public expenses, such as the cost of programs for young people and the rents for public clubs and hobby rooms. The board of directors of Tapiolan Lämpö Oy consists exclusively of representatives of the housing companies in Tapiola.

The supply companies in Tapiola formed an independent service company called Tapiolan Kunnallisteknillinen Huolto Oy, which is in charge of landscaping and grounds. This company also maintains flower beds. It is, as well, responsible for the collection and incineration of refuse and waste. It operates the sewer system, maintains roads and streets, and plows the snow in winter. The waste is transported to a special furnace located in the heating plant. Thus it is used to produce heat. For these services the owner of each dwelling unit pays a monthly fee, the so-called community-technical tariff. This system had to be employed because the rural municipality of Espoo was unwilling to assume the responsibility and the cost for these services. Tapiolan Sahkolaitos Oy is responsible for the distribution of electric current, which is a by-product of the central heating plant. The price for electricity in Tapiola is somewhat lower than in its surroundings but exactly the same as in Helsinki.

Once Tapiola is completed, its administration will be completely in the hands of residents who are experienced in its management. The Housing Foundation may thus turn with assurance to its next town projects.

The companies bill the consumers for the heat, hot water, or electricity they consume. Tariff rates are set and reconsidered annually at a general meeting of company stockholders. The service companies do more than perform services. They also own certain business premises and buildings, central garages, and a building in which the movie theater is located. In addition, the service companies are responsible for the offices of their managers, who are in charge of bookkeeping of all housing companies. They also collect rent and other payments for the housing companies, and they pay bills. Their income is derived from the housing companies in the form of tariffs. Additional income for the service companies is derived from the rents paid by the tenants of the business premises that the companies own and lease. The revenue of the service companies is derived from a house rental tax in addition to the heating tariff. The house rental tax was 0.10 Fmk per dwelling square meter per month in 1965. A leasing tax is another revenue source.

It is important to distinguish between the responsibility of services between Asuntosäätiö and the local government. Services such as hospitals, ambulance, fire department, and primary schools are provided by the municipality. However, the secondary schools were started by the parents of the schoolchildren with the help of Asuntosäätiö. A special body was established to finance the building and operations of the schools, banks, and insurance companies. It also is responsible for the state subsidy that covers the main part of the required capital.

As stressed before, Tapiola as an entity is the result of close and creative teamwork, strictly directed. In addition to architects, engineers, and highly skilled administrators, there have been economists, sociologists, landscape gardeners, home economists, and child and youth experts. To the names of the architects already listed, one should like to add some representatives of other professions, at least a few names among the most merited: Yrjo Riikonen, Chief of the Administrative Department of Asuntosäätiö; Viljo Suvanto and Lauri Niemi, Chief Engineers; Veikko Santala, Expert on Urban

Heating and Electric Works; Jussi Jännes and Carl-Johan Gottberg, Landscape Gardeners; and Uolevi Itkonen, Public Relations.

Tapiola's story is not without its humorous incidents. One of these concerned the conservation of a group of birch trees. Specific orders had been issued to save the trees; however, they were in the way of a temporary track used to support a moving crane. The crane was to be employed in the erection of a four-story prefab apartment house. In fact, the track and crane could have been set up on the opposite side of the house, avoiding the problem altogether, but the building engineers were stubborn and insisted on cutting down the trees. In order to be sure that the strict orders to save the birch trees would be followed, the Executive Director of the Housing Foundation used to be present in person at 7:00 A.M. when the work of the day started. However, the engineers were not about to lose the argument. One morning at 6:00 A.M., one hour before the ordinary start of work, they arrived with a commando group. All the trees were cut down. At 7:00 A.M. the boss arrived and noted that he had been beaten. He left without any comments, deciding to leave the matter to public opinion. It happened that those trees were a necessary foil to the apartment house's rather stark prefab facade and when the building was finished, the public criticized it vehemently. It was labeled ''the tractor factory,'' and the finger of guilt was pointed straight at the engineers. This treatment was repeated frequently over a considerable period of time. After that incident trees in Tapiola enjoyed greater affection. As for the building itself, the landscape department planted new trees, which have ful-filled the function of the original birches.

Another problem concerned a row of fountain jets in the town center's reflecting pool. The issue focused around the color of the underwater light that would illuminate the nighttime fountain display. Popular tastes favored multicolor illumination, but the purists preferred only white illumination. After loud and extended argument the question was passed to the administrators, who had to take the part of a Solomon. We ended with a ''both are best'' decision. The minutes of that particular meeting read as follows:

We shall execute both suggestions, as we have so often done in the past. The jets will be lit by white spots for three minutes to satisfy the architects and others of ''good'' taste. Then during the next three minutes the spots will change to all the colors of the rainbow to make the ordinary people happy. During these three minutes the architects can turn their backs on the pool and admire the architecture of Tapiola.

110 a,b,c.
Site details. The
finishing touches of
site development are
as much the product
of sensitive maintenance
as drafting-board concepts.

110 d,e,f,g.
Fun in Tapiola.

110 h,i, j,k.
Tapiola as a place
for rearing children
healthfully, in both
the physical and
social sense.

111.
Apartment buildings
designed by Marcus Tavio
in 1954 for young couples.
The balconies are convenient
for sunning babies, even
in winter.
112.
The variety and proximity
of different types of
residences in Tapiola.

113 a,b,c,d,e.
House interiors in Tapiola.

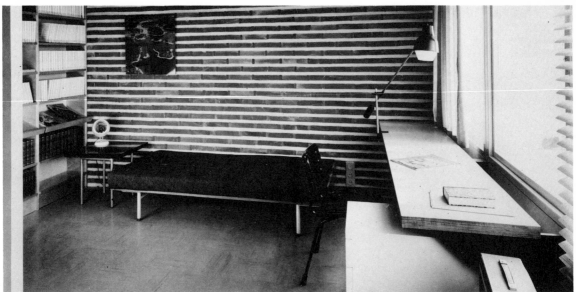

Provocation as a Tool in Creating a Town

There are two distinct steps in the creation of a
new town. Naturally, programming and planning
are vital, but realization of the plans is far more
difficult. Millions of words and hundreds of
books have been written on the subject. How
many thousands of excellent city plans have
been made during recent decades, decades during which relatively few new towns have been
built. It is a long and difficult way from planning
to realization. The builders of Tapiola are familiar
with these problems, and the problems are well
known to anyone who has dealt with projects in
actual practice. A few experiences should be
related.

Every time you want to make an important reform or present a farsighted project, you can expect to meet with stubborn conservatism and
deep prejudice. Not only are authorities conservative, so are public opinion and the press. Most
industrialists and businessmen think they are farsighted men of tomorrow. Among these men, in
fact, the percentage of conservatives is even
higher than the average of the public at large.
It is hard to believe, but it is true. It is such a
problem that you cannot realize a new town project without finding a remedy for this obstacle.
During the years in which Tapiola was built, it
was necessary to develop a method that might
be termed ''provocative town planning.'' In realizing our plans, we did not stop when con-
fronted by conservative resistance and prejudice.
If a condition for a move was lacking, we
created it if necessary by provocation, on our
own initiative, doing things and taking respon-

sibilities in a way that is not customary for planners or builders.

Asuntosäätiö did not want to build a dormitory town but rather a real community. Tapiola
had to have a vital economic life of its own, a
sufficient amount of jobs and a dynamic center
for business, administration, and cultural activities. The doors for all these activities were
opened by creating a planned town center and
two industrial areas within walking distances of
the residential units. It was expected that the
more farsighted industrialists and businessmen
would quickly discover the favorable conditions
offered to them. With the help of eloquent bro-
chures we told the industrial establishments, insurance companies, banks, and business people
that industrial sites were available in Tapiola. We
emphasized that the price was considerably
lower than in the city of Helsinki. New industry
could accommodate its workers a few hundred
yards from its plants in modern well-planned residential areas within a garden city environment.
There would no longer be a waste of spare time,
no traffic and parking problems, no air pollution.
The response to these opportunities was practically nil. The same happened when we had to
start to build the central tower in the town center
of Tapiola. It offered excellent business premises
and parking facilities as an alternative to offices
badly located in downtown Helsinki. From the
very beginning it was intended that the town
center of Tapiola would have high-quality attractions, good services, and first-class entertainment. A rooftop restaurant-cafe was planned for
the main administrative building. It would serve
both visitors and residents. However, in spite of
extensive searching we could not find one res-

taurant owner in Finland who was willing to assume the responsibility for either a restaurant or a cafe. It was then that we finally understood that it was necessary to take the ''provocative'' line in order to succeed in the creation of Tapiola Garden City. Planning and building of the town was not the only responsibility. It was also necessary to build up from nothing the whole economic life of the future town. And that, in fact, is exactly what happened.

We had already established, financed, and built Tapiolan Lämpö Oy, Tapiola's power plant. It provided heat, hot water, and electricity for 20,000 people. It was also the first major employer in Tapiola. Now we decided to build the first light-industry plant in Tapiola. This building, totally financed by Asuntosäätiö, was planned for twenty different enterprises. When the building was finished in 1961, we were unable to find any buyers for the premises, and so we rented them out. The tenants had the right to buy their premises in three years' time, after which we would be free to sell them. This worked extremely well; in a few years Asuntosäätiö had recovered all the capital invested in the light-industry building. We had also procured the first twenty enterprises, which represented a wide range of light industry: metal, electricity, wood, paper, plastics, and so forth. More important, mental resistance was broken. One of Finland's biggest printing offices, Weilin & Göös, decided to move the main part of their activity from Helsinki to Tapiola. They bought the two biggest sites available and started to build a plant that will offer jobs for about 700 people.

The story repeats itself in the case of the central administration tower in the town center. Asuntosäätiö planned, financed, and built it. Asuntosäätiö also took the responsibility for furnishing and decorating both the restaurant and cafeteria. Even the china and silver were provided before a restaurant manager was found. This man operated one of the leading downtown restaurants in Helsinki; he was an able organizer with lifelong experience in his field. Within a few years the restaurant and cafeteria were among the best in Finland. Yet, only three years earlier, the unanimous opinion held by restaurant owners was that this kind of restaurant could not succeed in Tapiola.

This procedure recurred many times during the building of Tapiola. So often business people and industrialists make calculations on the basis of limited experience and come to erroneous conclusions. What they regard as experience is often little more than conservatism and short-sightedness. They regard themselves as men of tomorrow, but too often they are men of yesterday. They calculate on the basis of existing conditions and circumstances, which they think will not change. The creator of a new town must be able to see which conditions and circumstances can be altered, and he must be prepared, unhappily, to provoke change himself, if necessary. At times he must depart quite radically from the usual procedures.

When the first inhabitants arrive in a new town, it is important to make life pulsate quickly. In order to achieve this, Asuntosäätiö had to establish and finance shopping centers, temporary school buildings, kindergartens, youth centers, and hobby rooms. Only fifteen months after the first inhabitants moved in, a cinema was opened. Without the help of Asuntosäätiö the waiting time for this important entertainment feature would have been very long indeed.

The story of Tapiola's elegant indoor-outdoor swimming hall in the town center is also typical of Asuntosäätiö's operations. We knew that this facility was badly needed and would add enormously to the activities of the town center. This type of public facility is usually the responsibility of the municipality. However, the plans for a swimming hall aroused heavy opposition in Espoo, in which municipality Tapiola belongs. The other districts in Espoo did not accept the idea because they had nothing like it. It was obvious that Tapiola would have to wait another ten years for a municipality-built pool, in spite of the fact that Tapiola had the largest population in Espoo and the greatest number of schoolchildren.

We had to act provocatively once again. Asuntosäätiö hired the best possible experts in the country and planned, financed, and built the entire structure. When the swimming hall was completed in 1965, Asuntosäätiö offered to sell the building for a moderate price to the municipality of Espoo. We were severely criticized, but the majority of the council of Espoo favored our offer and accepted it. Since then the swimming hall of Tapiola has had about 270,000 visitors each year and is listed as the most popular swimming hall in Finland.

The last major operation of this nature was the creation of "Heikintori," the combined activity center and department store in downtown Tapiola. Asuntosäätiö wanted to increase the capacity and level of service in the town center. In spite of the development of the town center into a business and cultural hub in a relatively short time, it was not quite satisfactory. A first-class department store was needed, one that could offer consumers the same variety of goods available in downtown Helsinki. As a goal we adopted the slogan, "Anything you can buy on Alexander Street (in downtown Helsinki), you will be able to find in the town center of Tapiola." But we did not want to build just an ordinary department store consisting of fifty to sixty specialty shops. We had several additional goals, too. In this building we wanted to concentrate many kinds of services, tourist entertainment, and premises for leisure activities. Furthermore, in this building we wanted to create the first covered shopping street in Finland. Our objective was a meeting place that would be totally independent of weather conditions. The planning of "Heikintori" started in 1963; the building was occupied in October 1968.

Once again, we found a new conception met with great hesitation on the part of the business world, but this time much enthusiasm was noticeable among the younger generation of business people. However, available outside backing was not sufficient, and Asuntosäätiö had to step in. Together with one of Finland's leading construction firms, Polar Oy, Asuntosäätiö established a corporation to finance and build Heikintori. Programming and planning was done by Asuntosäätiö's planning department. When Hei-

kintori was opened in October 1968, roughly 80
percent of its business premises had been sold.
The remaining ones were rented on short-term
leases.

 Plans have now been completed for an international hotel with restaurants, banquet halls, and
congress facilities. It will be located in the town
center on the southern side of the pool. It will
not be surprising if we find that we will need still
another provocative operation to transform this
project from an idea to a reality.

 The test of success of Asuntosäätiö's administration is to see Tapiola on the ground and to
consider again what the objectives were. The
basic intent was to build a modern cross-section
community, biologically healthful, rich in opportunity and choice, and close to nature. Apparently the buying public agreed with this aim.
In the fall of 1967, there were only 10 unsold
dwelling units in Tapiola, while greater Helsinki
had 2,000. Asuntosäätiö's experiment and
model seem to have made their point. Even before the end of the work in building Tapiola was
in sight, however, further objectives had come
into view—but these would never have occurred
in such fashion had not Tapiola paved the way.
In that adventure the key role of administration
was of the utmost importance. And probably the
principal lesson to be derived from Asuntosäätiö's operations is that great administrative skills
in urban planning are needed. This, in fact, is
of such importance that urban administrators
should be trained for this work professionally all
over the world.

114.
The swimming hall seen
from the roof of the central
tower building. The
swimming hall was designed
by Aarne Ervi.

115.
The swimming hall in warm
weather, with the glass
wall open.

116.
The swimming hall is one
of the most popular spots
in Tapiola for children.

4 Beyond Tapiola

The Seven Towns Plan

Tapiola is a story that started with the building
of a modern town at laboratory scale. During this
construction the conviction grew that good
urban planning must be correlated to good regional and even national planning. This led first
to the "seven towns" plan and then to the "Uusimaa 2010" plan.

When the planning and building of Tapiola
reached a halfway point, Asuntosäätiö began
drawing up the lines for its future work. From
the very beginning the purpose of Asuntosäätiö
was not just to build one town project, Tapiola.
Asuntosäätiö could operate over the whole
country, demonstrating new methods of housing
and pointing out new ways to plan and build
modern communities. Asuntosäätiö wanted to
prove more than that its ideals could be realized
in practice—it wanted to offer to people in need
of housing and jobs a real choice in ways of
planning and building communities.

Tapiola had been planned at laboratory scale to
avoid excessive risk; the problems were easier to
manage if the project was not too big. The experience in Tapiola showed that the next town project has to be bigger. It had also become clear
that the optimum size for an independent town
unit, at least in southern Finland, would be
about 100,000 inhabitants. In some special
cases it might possibly be 200,000. The lines
for Asuntosäätiö's work in the future were drawn
according to these realizations. Valuable information was obtained from future population projections and from investigations of the migration
from rural areas to towns. These population studies had been made by Väestöpoliittinen Tutki-
muslaitos (The Population Research Institute) in
the late 1940s. They indicated that the Uusimaa region would become a zone of strong
population pressure. In the spring of 1959, The
National Planning Office (Valtakunnan Suunnit-
tely Foimisto) published its findings on population development and manpower resources in
Finland during the years 1950 to 1970. This
was followed by a 1964 publication of population development in Finnish communities from
1960 to 1990. All these investigations proved
that the urban population upsurge was gathering
momentum. Simultaneously, Helsinki was suffer-
ing from a shortage of suitable sites, a sharp rise
in land prices, and ever-increasing congestion
from traffic.

When the results of this research were analyzed
at the planning department of Asuntosäätiö, we
were ready for the next move. It was decided
that preparations for future land acquisition
should be made well ahead and for a long-term
view. Consequently, Asuntosäätiö purchased the
Störsvik estate in Siuntio in 1960 and the Stensvik area in Espoo in 1961. This was followed by
the acquisition of Dåvits estate in Kirkkonummi
in 1962.

All these actions were accepted in due order by
the Council of Asuntosäätiö, where the six large
national organizations were represented (The Finnish Family Welfare League, The Confederation
of Finnish Trade Unions, The Union of Civil Servants, The Central Association of Tenants, The
Finnish Association of Disabled Civilians and Ex-
servicemen, and The General Mannerheim Child
Welfare League).

One cannot start planning new towns without at least the most vital portions of land. But it is even more important to purchase the necessary land in the right geographical places—with the help of population and economic studies.

Naturally, both the preparatory research work and land acquisition had to be done quietly. Once that was done, however, we had to give publicity to the new projects. This was difficult. We felt that we would cause a shock, possibly even greater than when Tapiola was announced in the early 1950s. Another consideration had to be taken into view. That was to protect Asuntosäätiö itself from possibly stormy public assault. In particular it was important to avoid the charge of utopianism.

As Executive Director of Asuntosäätiö and as the chief of its planning department, I published my "Seven Towns Plan" privately in 1962. Its objective was to propose a solution to urban sprawl around Helsinki. The seven towns plan was first published in Suomen Kuvalehti, one of Finland's main illustrated magazines. The plan was discussed further and in more elaborate form in a bulletin called Valtakunnansuunnittelu (National Planning), for which I was the editor-in-chief.

The plan proposed setting a limit on the size of Helsinki and a way of absorbing Helsinki's population increase as well as migrants from middle or northern Finland over the next fifteen to twenty years. The seven-new-towns plan was not proposed as the last word in national planning. To curb the one-way migration to southern Finland, the plan proposed that the government start a balanced decentralization of industry, administration, and cultural facilities by every pos-

sible means. The plan also suggested improving the most underdeveloped areas beyond the Helsinki region. To do this, three completely new towns should be founded: one in northern Finland, one in Ostrobothnia, and one in eastern Finland. Alternatively, a twin town could be built adjacent to certain existing communities. Of the seven new towns in Uusimaa, none would be more than thirty minutes by rail or road from Helsinki, thus enabling that city to play its proper role as capital. The towns themselves would be surrounded by open land or water. Only by the creation of these new towns could Finland prepare itself for the dynamic social changes that will occur in the next ten to fifteen years. This period will witness a swing away from agriculture to industry, and prosperity will hinge on that swing. Forestry, too, will decrease its labor needs. The manpower thus freed must be placed in sound, productive industry and trade that will occur mainly in urbanized areas.

The seven towns plan did not receive much attention at first. Some of its opponents tried to kill it through silence, but a year later the picture changed. Through the initiative of the Architectural League of New York City, a Tapiola exhibition was opened in October 1963 in New York. All material for this exhibition was prepared by Asuntosäätiö. To that exhibition was added a section wherein certain aspects of the seven towns plan were presented. At the time a UN delegation from Finland and some Finnish journalists were visiting New York. The result was major news stories complete with large headlines in the Finnish press. Then, instead of silence we found ourselves in the midst of con-

troversy and publicity, which is just what was needed.

The next move was an exhibition organized by Asuntosäätiö in Helsinki in the spring of 1965. The exhibition was called "Tapiola and the Province of Uusimaa, 1965." This exhibition included much of the same material as the Tapiola Exhibition in New York. (In the meantime, it had been transformed into a traveling exhibit that traveled throughout the United States over a three-year period.) In the Uusimaa section of the exhibit we presented the regional and local planning problems of the province of Uusimaa and the capital city of Helsinki. As a counterproposition to the seven towns plan we gave publicity to a rival plan, an official plan for the Helsinki area that had been prepared but until then not published by Helsingin Seutukaavaliitto (the Helsinki Area Planning Association). This plan became known as the "amoeba" plan, with obvious reference to its form—or lack of it. The Helsinki Area Planning Association proposed a typical radiocentric plan, in which the population would depend on improved transportation facilities. We were highly critical of this plan. First we felt that a million and a half people would be crammed into narrow wedges between future highways. In our view it was inexcusable to concentrate people in this fashion in Europe's most sparsely settled country. Second, a population settled in a uniformly dense and sprawling pattern—with no coordination in development and land use and with no coordination between planning, residences, and jobs—would mean complete dependence on Helsinki for employment, recreation, and services. Third, population would be concentrated along the main highways lead-

ing to Helsinki. Hundreds of thousands of people would be exposed to the danger, noise, and exhaust of day-long traffic—a situation that was entirely unnecessary, for through traffic and residential areas ought to be kept apart. Fourth, much of this population would be separated from the Gulf of Finland and its archipelago, unquestionably the most valuable area in Uusimaa for recreation. Fifth, the benefits of the coast and harbor areas—vital to Finland's national development—would go untapped.

The seven towns plan was conceived for the purpose of realizing modern principles of town and country planning in the province of Uusimaa and in order to avoid the inevitable problems of the "amoeba" plan. It would accomplish a number of benefits.

The population of the Helsinki metropolitan region, estimated at 1,545,000 in the plan of the Helsinki Area Planning Association, would be kept to a maximum of 1,300,000. As a result, and assuming government action, the pressure of population in Uusimaa would be eased by approximately 250,000 people, to the advantage of the population centers and communities inland. Thus Helsinki would be spared excessive and needless centralization and the risk of destructive change. A ceiling would be set for the growth of the city. The maximum population for the city proper would not be allowed to exceed 630,000, which could be accomplished by several means, including a plan to limit building volume in the central city.

The developing areas on the coastal districts of Uusimaa would be made into independent communities. Every community would include dwellings, jobs, and cultural and commercial centers, serving the whole population as whole towns. Some of the new communities would be built on virgin ground, where modern planning principles could be achieved according to economic and social criteria, as in Tapiola. Other communities would be built around existing centers, assuming that the planning of the land would not be obstructed by existing patterns of site ownership and assuming that the original centers could be adopted and absorbed into a new development design.

Preliminary investigations indicated that the locations of the larger communities suggested here would be best in the regions of Tapiola, Espoo Bay, and Porkkala, in central Uusimaa in the vicinity of Lohja and Riihimäki-Hyvinkää, and in eastern Uusimaa in the vicinity of Porvoo and Loviisa.

Large open areas would be retained among all the communities, new and old. This open land would constitute approximately 90 percent of the total area of Uusimaa. It would be placed under the protection of the law and used for agriculture, forestry, and recreation. Those areas with the greatest beauty, with the greatest cultural and historical value, would be preserved. The large green belts would have well-kept forests, cultivated land, and miniature communities, where the old peasant village and mill traditions would be fostered. Nearby town dwellers would thus be able to enjoy them as vital and precious recreational resources. In addition, the new towns would constitute profitable markets because of their purchasing power. They would offer entirely new opportunities for the economic and cultural development of the surrounding countryside. The ruin of the countryside in Uusimaa by excessive building pressure would be prevented. Further, a destructive, unmanageable, and undesirable wave of formless urban growth would be avoided, and converted instead into an opportunity to create humane and livable cities.

1.
A model of Tapiola, built for
the special exhibit "Tapiola
and the Province of Uusimaa,
1965." The view is looking
southeastward.

2.
The information pavilion at the
town center entrance. The
model is on display inside the
pavilion.

3.
This concept resembles
an amoeba in form and
would repeat, the errors
of growth of industrial
cities the world over.

◯ Neighborhood
◯ Suburban area
◯ Group of suburban areas
▦ Industrial area
▦ Special-purpose area
0.0 Estimated future population,
1000's.

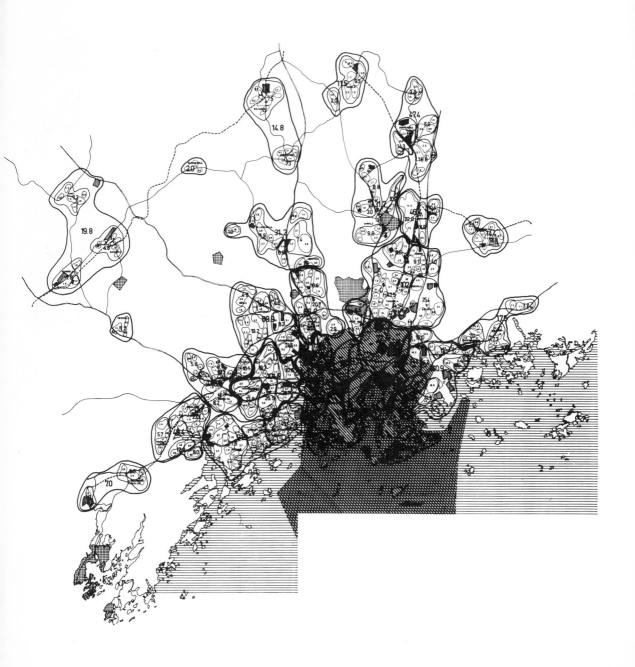

4.
The Seven Towns plan.
5.
The plan showing Porkkala
and Espoo Bay, with the industrial sectors.

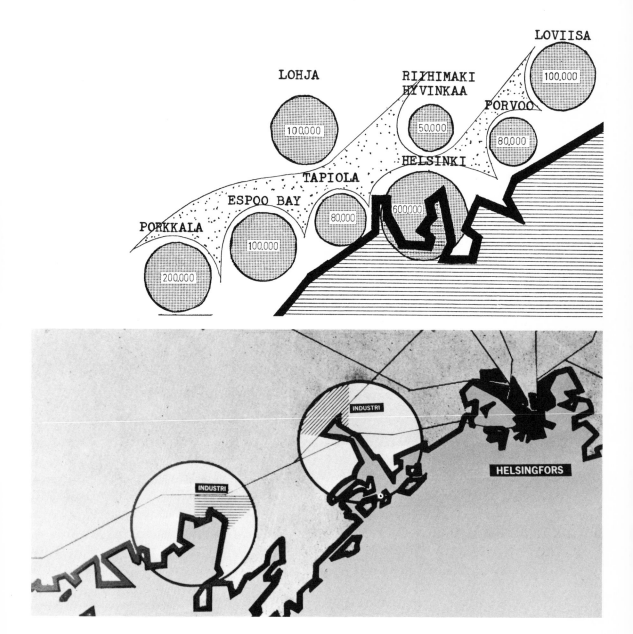

6.
The site for Porkkala. Based
on the lessons thus far
learned in Tapiola, this site
is being developed, its own
character preserved, but
made an everyday habitat,
not a weekend retreat.

7.
Espoo Bay.
8.
Espoo Bay. The model
view of Fig. 10 is from
the same angle.

9.
The Twin City on Espoo Bay

The proposed twin city on Espoo Bay will be located on both sides of the inlet. The conditions for planning a new town are excellent: the highway westward from Helsinki; the electrified railroad to Kirkkonummi, already in operation; a constantly expanding and dynamic industrial area on both sides of this railroad from Kauklahti in Espoo to Masala in Kirkkonummi. This area will be the main source of employment for the inhabitants of the beautifully located residential areas on both sides of the bay. The distance between home and place of employment will be only one to three miles. Additional employment will be offered by three more light industrial areas— Kivenlahti and Suomenoja in Espoo and the Båtvik area in Kirkkonummi. Downtown Helsinki lies only 11 miles from the bay.

It is hard to think of a more attractive and human location for a modern town. The components are the Gulf of Finland with its beautiful archipelago and the inlet of Espoo Bay, penetrating deep into the mainland and dividing the city into two parts. In addition, the planners have one lake and three beautiful "lagoons" at their disposal, each with a future village center of its own. For the traffic inside the city there are two circular roads, an inner and an outer circle. The latter leads to an admirably situated water sports center on the island of Pentala. This will serve yachting and other seabound activities.

There are few urban sites in the entire world with this concentration of advantages.

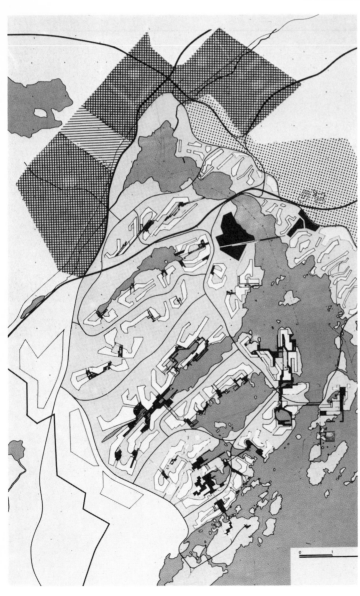

10.
Model of Aalto's plan for the
eastern side of Espoo Bay.
11.
Plan for the eastern portion
of the Espoo Bay area,
designed by Alvar Aalto
in 1966.

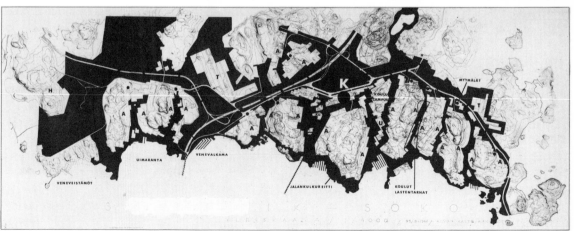

"Uusimaa 2010"

Thanks to the "Tapiola and Uusimaa 1965" Exhibition, public debate over urbanization and urban planning started in earnest in Finland. We had indeed caused a real shock, but the state of passive silence had definitely been broken. The opposition to our concept was based mainly on the argument that Asuntosäätiö intended to build dormitory towns that would lack the economic prerequisites of active communities. Asuntosäätiö was well aware that these arguments were groundless and that they arose from a lack of knowledge of the facts. Nevertheless, it was felt that both the authorities and the press should be furnished with more detailed reports by experts on the issues under debate. The need was felt to be all the greater because there had been virtually no investigations of this nature performed in Finland to date. Accordingly, the board of Asuntosäätiö decided to appoint a working group of eight experts of wide experience to study the problems in the planning of the Province of Uusimaa.

The following points were included in the instructions given by Asuntosäätiö to the group of experts, who were headed by Lassi Iharvaara, M.Tech.Sc., and Matti Tausti, architect.

1. Real communities must be planned that can offer, in addition to dwellings, the highest degree of job opportunities and centers for business and the service trades. There must be, as well, facilities for the recreational and cultural pursuits of the inhabitants. In all these facilities the requirements will be considerably higher than in Tapiola.

2. These new communities cannot be planned correctly unless their character, future population, and economic and industrial basis are known, at least in outline. This applies in particular to the centers of the future communities.

3. It is necessary to emphasize the division of work among various communities. The tasks pertaining to one unit cannot be defined without simultaneously viewing it as a part of the larger unit. For example, the traffic problems of a particular community cannot be solved successfully unless the size and character of the other communities that are being created or developed in the proximity are known.

4. It is of special importance to establish the water supply system of the new communities and its connections with neighboring areas and the whole country. Without these investigations the planning problems cannot be resolved successfully. The Finnish government commissioned (in 1966) the Board of Roads and Waterways to prepare a water supply plan for south Finland, but no corresponding plan for the disposal of effluence is being undertaken. All studies, general or regional, that can hasten the solution of these problems, at least within a few years, will save considerable sums of public money and help to avoid fatal mistakes in planning.

5. In the Porkkala area, the question of maritime activities—seafaring and harbors—will dominate the planning and development of the whole community. Whether Porkkala is to have one harbor or more, whether it will be a local special harbor or a national general one, are questions that must be answered as soon as possible if serious mistakes in planning are to be avoided.

In August 1965, the University of Pennsylvania New Towns Seminar visited and studied Tapiola for five days. The members of this seminar included outstanding planning officials and many prominent representatives of American universities. Before Tapiola the seminar had been in Scotland and in the Stockholm region. Upon departure seven members of the seminar delivered written statements to the Finnish press. One of the statements was given by Mr. C. McKim Norton, then president of the Regional Planning Association of New York and a member of the National Capital Planning Commission in Washington, D.C. Said Mr. Norton,

As a regional planner for the New York Metropolitan area this visit to Helsinki . . . has been a memorable and inspiring experience. Helsinki stands today where New York stood about 75 years ago, when New York started to explode into its environs. Uusimaa Province is, relatively speaking, in its frontier stage of urban growth. All ways of settlement are open to it, and the next decade or two are crucial ones in which irrevocable decisions must be made.

Fortunately there is vision and leadership at this important moment in Finland's urban history. Tapiola Garden City is a living example of one way Uusimaa Province can meet its future. In Tapiola Finns can experience a sample, as it were, of low-density urban living at its very best.

Mr. von Hertzen's seven towns plan for the next stage of Uusimaa Province's urban growth is also most interesting and appealing. Like Tapiola, it is an obtainable objective. Unlike some new towns plans which turn their back on the old central city, the von Hertzen proposal would create a genuine metropolitan area with its focus on Helsinki for central government and commercial and cultural functions while allowing those activities that are not essentially central to disperse.

If central Helsinki can be but 30 minutes by rail or bus from any of the seven new or expanded towns proposed by Mr. von Hertzen, the metropolitan city of well over a million envisaged for the year 2000 and beyond will combine human scale living with urbanity in a way no other city of this magnitude has ever achieved.

The seven towns proposal was built upon broad concepts. It had not been subjected to detailed scrutiny so as to probe its premises in depth and explore its suggestions. Accordingly, on December 11, 1964, the Housing Foundation signed a contract for a preliminary master plan and a background investigation. This was published as a booklet in May 1967, titled *Uusimaa 2010.** The "Uusimaa 2010" plan provided the needed scrutiny and confirmed the broad principles of the seven towns plan. It also led to inevitable alterations in the seven towns plan. These alterations were largely due to refinements, quantifications, and precise adjustments. The broad principles still hold, but in somewhat modified form.

The year chosen as a target date coincided with the target year used in other studies. The scope of the plan is indicated by the disciplines represented in its preparation. These included regional planning, urban design, transportation, marine engineering, water usage, demography, business, regional geography, architecture, public school planning, public administration, climatology, and public health.

* *Uusimaa 2010* (Uusimaa Plan), Oy Tilgmann Ab, Helsinki 1967. (The book includes an English summary and picture captions in English.)

In *Uusimaa 2010,* it was noted that the then-current division of greater Helsinki into four planning districts was untenable, that the entire Uusimaa province had to be considered as a whole, and that the development potential of all of Finland had to be considered in order for any meaningful plans for Uusimaa to be made. The plan for the year 2010 studied several possible systems of urban communities, their location, size, area of influence, relationships, and traffic needs. Insights were gained as to the usage of general land areas. Studies were made of administration, schools, hospitals, harbors, transportation networks, water resources, and waste disposal.

A number of possible models were developed, and from these the team of experts selected the most advantageous. The nature of their work made it difficult to analyze the models quantitatively. Thus mathematical evaluations were not allowed to dominate. The broad spectrum of concerns entertained by the study team and their systematic evaluation were felt to be superior to the possible deficiencies of determination by mathematical evaluations.

When the team started work, they were instructed to observe several principles. First, Asuntosäätiö was interested in building whole, viable, urban communities, not dormitory towns. Second, no sound planning for communities could be done without up-to-date information on future population and economic and industrial activity. Third, all town plans would have to be based on a valid picture of their roles in their regional or national contexts. Fourth, the programming of water, waste disposal, and highway planning would derive from regional information.

Fifth, a careful investigation of harbor facilities and needs was required, particularly in the Porkkala area. That area has the greatest potential for new harbor development, which would relieve pressure on Helsinki.

The Uusimaa 2010 plan confirmed the seven towns plan, but it added considerable refinement, needed quantification and precision on numerous essential details. In essence, it emphasized that the starting point for a study of Uusimaa's future was a study and projection of Finland's future. This would be a future, as has been pointed out, characterized by urbanization and a decline of some of the small, rural towns.

The essence of the Uusimaa 2010 plan is, first of all, to divide the entire country into eight administrative regions. These, of course, are rational political-economic-geographic-administrative divisions. The southernmost of the provinces, Uusimaa, is then treated as eight portions. Of these the Helsinki metropolitan region is dominant. Finally, the Helsinki metropolitan region, too, is divided into eight portions. The predominant one is, of course, Helsinki, but it is complemented by seven towns, including Tapiola. Overall, then, Uusimaa 2010 is a rational plan for all of Finland, starting at national scale but getting down into the fine detail of particular towns.

Thus one of the main modifications of the
seven towns plan was a somewhat different regional role than earlier imagined for Porkkala
and Espoo Bay. It was correct to suppose that
Porkkala might become one of the major new
towns in the Uusimaa pattern, as well as
Espoonlahti (Espoo Bay)—but the latter would
function as one of the town units composing the
Helsinki metropolitan area. The essence of the
difference between the seven towns idea and
the Uusimaa 2010 plan was that the seven
towns became seven subregions, each comprised of one or more towns in a satellite
relationship.

The idea of relieving Helsinki of all overburden
of growth seemed feasible. So did the idea of a
regional pattern of open space. So, too, did the
rationale of scheduling major public works, like
roads, waters, and harbors, to give foundation to
the plan. Porkkala would serve a main function
as a new port, relieving Helsinki's overburdened
facilities and avoiding the crowding of Helsinki's
streets with the transit shipments of marine
merchandise.

13.
A national plan of
administration. Eight
provinces. (from "Uusimaa
2010")

14.
The province of Uusimaa
with eight administrative
units. (from "Uusimaa
2010")

15.
Metropolitan Helsinki: The
capital city plus seven
town units. (from "Uusimaa
2010")

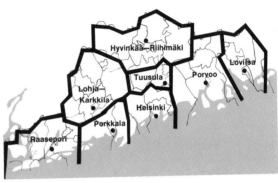

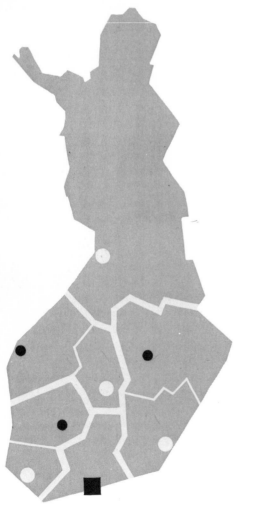

16.
The Seven Towns concept
in the Uusimaa area. This
is the alternative to the
"amoeba" plan.

- ▬ Urban center
- ● Urban area
- ▥ Recreation
- ═ National highway
- — Main road
- ······· Railroad

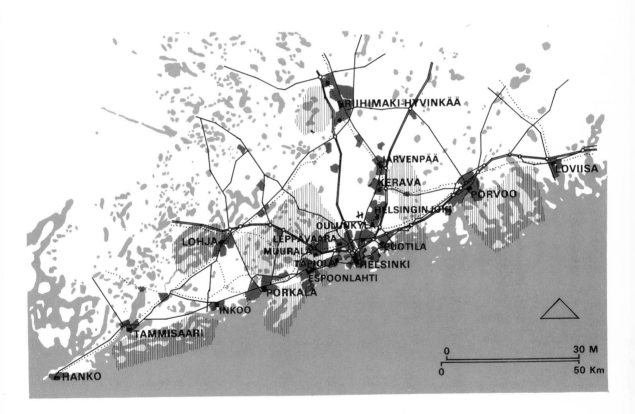

17.
Uusimaa 2010.
The seven towns concept
originally conceived in 1962
has become, through careful
study, a plan for seven
subregions in Uusimaa, each
with a major urban center.

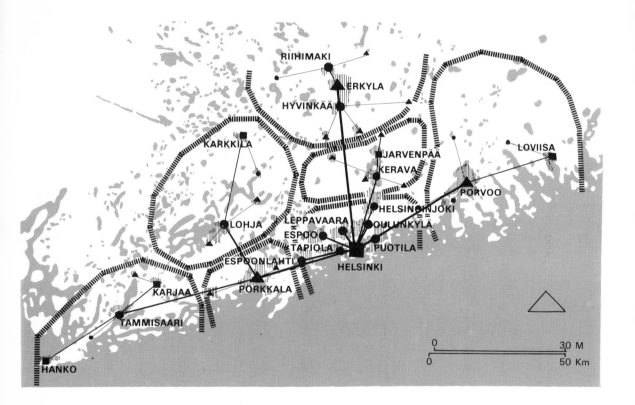

■   Primary and secondary centers

◤   Tertiary centers, with direct access to Helsinki

●◞   A fourth-order center

◪   A fifth-order center

◢   A sixth-order center

•   A seventh-order center

‖‖‖   Outline of a subregion. There are seven of these.

18.

A rational regional plan for Uusimaa will mean a more tenable and a happier relation of people to land. This plan shows urban areas in relation to regional open space. Here we have the full development of the old garden city idea but developed to its modern state. The "new towns" are the basic entities of an urbanized region wherein settlements and nature complement each other.

19a,b,c,d.
A rational regional plan
means that the older
picturesque areas have a
chance to survive because
they will be neither drained
of their local economics nor
impacted by development.
They will be able to continue
to thrive as viably contrasting
environments to the new
regional urbanization, and
they will be part of that
regional pattern.

Uusimaa in 1968

The background investigation on Uusimaa 2010 was published in May 1967 and presented to the Prime Minister and the Minister of the Interior. It was also presented to the President of the Republic, Mr. Urho Kekkonen.

Until now the Uusimaa 2010 plan has not been accepted by any authority whatsoever. However, the facts and trends presented in it could hardly be ignored. The regional and urban pattern of Uusimaa 2010 has also proved to be far superior to every other suggestion presented by the end of 1968. This also applies to the latest suggestions made by the Helsinki Area Planning Association in 1968.

In spite of the fact that only a year and a half has elapsed since *Uusimaa 2010* was published, remarkable things have already happened. By decision of the Finnish Government two municipalities, Hyvinkää and Lohja, which were both designated as new towns in the seven towns plan, have been declared incorporated towns starting in 1969. The council of the municipality of Espoo, to which Tapiola belongs, has adopted a preliminary general plan according to which Tapiola will be a regional center for a town unit of 80,000 inhabitants. According to this same adopted plan another town unit, Kivenlahti (70,000 inhabitants), will be created on the eastern shore of the Espoo Bay. This means that the first half of the proposed twin city in Espoo Bay is already a reality. The time when the corresponding measures for the second part are taken (the western shore of Espoo Bay, which is located in the municipality of Kirkkonummi), depends to a limited extent on the municipalities

of Kirkkonummi and Siuntio. These are agricultural areas and quite conservative. They have yet to accept the facts of life of modern urbanization. The same applies to the Porkkala seaside town.

However, industrialization and urbanization are approaching these areas at an accelerating pace. The construction of a new highway from Helsinki westward has already reached the Storsvik area in Porkkala. The electrified railroad from Helsinki to Kirkkonummi was opened in the beginning of 1969. A dynamic industrial area on both sides of this railroad from Kauklahti in Espoo to Masala in Kirkkonummi is growing up. This area will be the main source of employment for the beautifully located residential areas on both sides of Espoo Bay. No opposition, however stubborn, can prevent the new town of Espoo Bay from being a reality by the end of the 1970s.

As a matter of fact, it is already under construction. In order to facilitate the creation of the next new town project, Espoo Bay, Asuntosäätiö offered to collaborate with two other organizations: Keskus-SATO, another large nonprofit housing cooperative, and Polar Ltd., one of the biggest construction firms. Like Asuntosäätiö, these two organizations were landowners on the western shore of Espoo Bay that was called Lounaisrannikko, on the southwest coast. In 1966, two important agreements were signed. In the first one Asuntosäätiö, Keskus-SATO, and Polar established a body—the Southwest Coast Consortium—to act as a tool for realizing the southwest coast project, the first part of the new town of Espoo Bay. The second agreement was made between the Consortium and the municipality of

Espoo, according to which the Consortium accepted responsibility for the financing of site improvements in the area. Strict rules were established in order to ensure the necessary number of jobs, a balanced social structure, and good services. The municipality agreed to review the general plan as well as to prepare the town plan according to an efficient schedule.

In 1968, the site plan for the first neighborhood of 10,000 inhabitants was approved. The corresponding part of the water and sewage system was completed, as well as the urban heating system. The streets and roads were ready, the schools and kindergartens under planning. Early in 1969, about 1,200 dwellings were completed. The first inhabitants of the southwest coast had started their pioneering urban life. The new town on the shore of Espoo Bay had started to be a reality.

According to the Uusimaa 2010 plan, the metropolitan area of Helsinki should comprise present-day Helsinki, municipalities of Espoo and Kauniainen, the rural commune of Helsinki, and parts of Kirkkonummi and Sipoo. To the west of the city area of Helsinki four independent town units were envisaged. Three of these (Tapiola, Leppävaara, and Muurala) were totally, and the fourth one (Espoo Bay/Kivenlahti) partly, situated in the muncipality of Espoo. According to the Uusimaa plan the administration of the Helsinki metropolitan area should be organized in such a way that activities of lower category are managed by those urban units responsible primarily for the matters affecting their own population. In order to obtain ideas for a new administrative town center for the town unit Muurala, the municipality of Espoo extended an invitation to an international competition in 1966. According to estimates there would be 90,000 inhabitants in the immediate sphere of influence of the center in the objective date of the competition. The competition did not aim at a final solution of the town plan but at illustrating various possible ways of creating a town center in the competition area. The closing date of the competition was June 10, 1967. Altogether there were 172 entries in this competition. It was won by a team of Polish architects and planners.

Thus an extremely dynamic activity has taken place during a period of six years starting in 1962 by the presentation in public of the seven towns plan.

20a, b, c, d.
Architectural details in
Tapiola.

21a, b, c, d.
Site and landscaping details
in Tapiola.

22a, b, c, d.
People enjoying Tapiola.

23a, b, c, d.
Paths in Tapiola.

5 The
Lessons of
Tapiola

A Philosophy for New Towns*

Since the industrial revolution many of the official premises of town planning—if one can speak of such in the present chaos—have been in error. As a result of bad judgment, bad investments have been made in every country, each more disastrous than the last. Nevertheless, the financial resources needed to build good and biologically suitable towns and communities were and still are available. The only hindrance has been and is a lack of intelligence and ability to organize. Planning and building a new town means a continuous fight against all kinds of conservatism, prejudice, local self-interest, and plain ignorance. It is infuriating to hear the mayors of old cities, cities that can offer their inhabitants only inconvenience and discomfort, proclaim, "Right or wrong, whether our city is good or bad, we need the existing taxpayers and will fight to the death any scheme to attract them away." A city or town should exist for people, not vice versa. If old cities fail, we need to make new ones. In fact, only by making new ones can we begin to solve the problems of the old ones.

It is no accident that a modern city is a place where it is oppressive to work, even more difficult to move around in, and almost intolerable to live in. The sad fact is that hardly any metropolis in the world can offer its inhabitants the commodity they absolutely require as human beings: fresh air. First-class drinking water,

* This section was adapted from an article entitled "Finanz-wirtschaftliche Aspekte für das Bauwesen" by Heikki von Hertzen in a special issue of CONSTRUCTA II of Deutsche Messe und Ausstellungs-AG, Hanover, 1967, and used with their permission.

many good residential areas, many workplaces, many leisure-time places, nighttime quiet, and unpolluted waters are also luxuries that cities with supposedly high standards of living are generally unable to provide.

Examining these problems from the point of view of economics, one can clearly see that we have misled ourselves into creating urban situations which, despite justification from a so-called economic point of view, reveal that the most expensive methods of building towns have been followed. When overconcentration occurs, it means just this. In the United States, with a present population of nearly 200 million, 70 percent of the people live in an area that geographically represents only 1 percent of the whole country. The remaining 30 percent of the people occupy 99 percent of the area of the country. How, by any measure, can this be regarded as good sense? If one takes the corresponding figures in Scandinavia, the same quandary presents itself. Yet history shows the way from overcentralization to a new order of urban structure. In its day, centralization was needed and was important, being justified for reasons of safety and efficiency as well as for economy and administration. However, when it reached a certain limit, its drawbacks began exceeding its advantages. People were not intelligent enough to realize when this took place. But now we ought to be sufficiently perceptive to see where a better course lies. We have to discover when and where we should centralize or restructure, as well as what to centralize or restructure. Both are needed; both are methods by which suitable surroundings are created for man—but centralization alone should not dominate.

Often one hears debates on the subject: Should we build new towns or rebuild the old ones? It is obvious that we have to do both. The rebuilding of old cities is necessary because so much human effort is invested there, and its results still reside there. But one cannot hope to tackle the problems of the old cities without making new ones that siphon off some of the pressure to overbuild. The world will not be able to make good human environments for its people if it relies solely on the old cities, expanded or made more crowded. That would be simply illogical and should not be done. When building new cities in virgin country, one can solve the most intricate problems of urban design much better than in the old cities where one is tied up by so many existing arrangements. Furthermore, an extensive new towns program gives the urban renewal effort additional time and latitude. Overly rapid growth in the old cities makes it impossible to undertake renewal without causing more problems. We cannot do without good planning, but good planning needs a fair opportunity in order to succeed. The value of real experience as a test of theory is summarized by what has been done in Tapiola and what was learned from this experiment.

In Finland, Asuntosäätiö tried to solve these acute problems in theory and in practice. The problem of modern town planning cannot be solved on a theoretical plane alone. Only by building subsequent to research and by evaluating the results can theory have any meaning. An experiment of this kind was made in Finland by building the garden city of Tapiola. Of course, in presenting Tapiola no assertion is made that it should be copied blindly. One would be foolish

to copy it in Arizona or the South of France. In every part of the earth towns should grow from topography, climate, and local character. New towns should be created to respond to the indigenous way of life.

There can be no healthy economy without good national health. If planning causes damage to human health, it cannot be deemed to be economical. On the other hand, one might ask whether many urban solutions today can be regarded as economical at all. Can traffic on three levels cost only three times as much as traffic on one? Might it not cost eight or ten times as much? Might not many traffic arrangements, artificial illumination, and air conditioning render the so-called economics of modern cities illusory? Asuntosäätiö's view is that concentrated and dense building is an extremely expensive method, whereas suitably chosen and spaciously planned communities are an economically profitable method. If experiments similar to Tapiola were carried out in various locales, their results would confirm these conclusions.

Consider this example: Suppose that 300,000 to 500,000 new inhabitants are to be placed either in the area of a present city or by building an entirely new town where suitable premises can be found. Based on Asuntosäätiö's experience, an impartial investigation would soon show that placing this number of inhabitants within the area of a big exciting city, or even in its vicinity, would be considerably more expensive. Sociologically, the result would be much poorer than if a new community were built, constructed without the limitations prevailing in existing towns. Considerable savings could be made in the traffic net and vehicular storage

areas alone. Streets with heavy traffic, express-ways, and viaducts are extremely expensive. Similarly, the cost of parking space in multistory parking buildings is often much greater than the price of the vehicles they house.

Asuntosäätiö experimented with a new housing policy and a new method of town planning over a period of almost fifteen years. The work is al-most complete, except for a part of the town center, which will require several years to finish. The experiment in Tapiola has been deliberately kept on a small scale. The city is a modern com-munity built on a laboratory scale to gain suf-ficient experience and at the same time to avoid unnecessary risks. Now it is time to take the next steps. It used to be that town location was tied to transportation routes, mainly because of in-dustrial siting that requires rail and road sys-tems. That is still true to an extent, but not nearly to the extent of former times. Even in-dustry is not the determinant it once was. The modern city has other ''basic'' functions, such as education, administration, services and, in-creasingly, leisure and recreation.

In 1962, the seven towns plan was published. It covered the overall planning of the surround-ings of Helsinki and the most important province of Finland, Uusimaa. It was based on the propo-sition that good dwellings for people cannot be built unless these dwellings are placed in a well-planned urban milieu. There can be no housing policy without close collaboration with town planning. Further, a town plan cannot be made without knowledge of what will happen in its surroundings and in the neighboring towns. Thus there can be no efficient town planning without efficient regional planning—and the lat-ter is not possible without overall national plan-ning. Both are to a very great degree economic problems. When the change is made from the present method of improvisation to well-governed methods of nationwide overall plan-ning, regional planning, and town planning, vast sums of money will be saved. These savings can be used to create a more workable and more beautiful urban milieu. Only when planning has been brought to this level will it be able to solve the problems of air, water, and soil pollution, and to subject traffic to the service of man. ''The ability to limit reveals the master.''

We should also be impatient with the specula-tor-businessman who evaluates everything in terms of monetary profits and with the bureau-crat who evaluates in terms of statistics. Neither method can build the optimal human environ-ment. The worst businessmen are the ones who think only in terms of profit, and the worst ad-ministrators those who think only in terms of sta-tistics. The job of businessman and administrator is to create the conditions whereby good plans can be realized. You do not go to the minister of culture to get a symphony, nor do you go to the ministry of the interior to get a new town. It is not their job to create these works. It is their job to ensure that conditions exist whereby these things can be accomplished.

Tapiola had to be constructed by a private foundation rather than a public agency or municipal government. A private foundation necessarily has to stress administrative efficiency, economy, and accomplishment. It is not under pressure to make a maximum profit, as a private business enterprise would be. It also takes a private foundation to initiate innovation of this kind. Government, through its congress or parliament, should not wait to take directives from its constituents, the public, for they are not aware of the possibilities that lie dormant within its capabilities. People cannot be enlightened with a paper plan; they need a living model to judge. Therefore, many experimental towns must be built so that people can decide from real models what they prefer. Five percent of every country's building budget should be spent producing those models. Only then can progress occur.

These lessons hold for the urban problems of all urbanizing countries. In modern housing the elemental unit of planning is no longer the house or even the block but a housing area or a part of a town. Only inside the framework of this more complicated social structure can the social necessities of a community be realized. Variety within these areas is essential, for it prevents monotony and facilitates the mixture of different types of people. Big housing schemes for special groups, of whatever income level, should be avoided. Proper social composition can be best achieved by a mixture of different types of housing, by providing a variety of workplaces, careful allocation of dwelling units, and public information. Dwellings and jobs should be placed in reasonable proximity.

Subsidized housing should be equal to normal housing. While all attempts should be made to reduce costs, a false economy should not be realized by cutting things down to a minimum, either dwelling areas or fittings. Standards of living are rising, and minimal housing quickly becomes obsolete. This applies as well to surroundings, which are essential components of residential areas. The house provides only a quarter of what a family requires. A question as to the form of subsidy arises: Should it go to the individual or to programs? Both seem necessary. Individual aid, that is, direct subsidy payments, counteract some of the injustices inherent in general programs. They can also be readjusted continuously to changing family needs, and so offer flexibility. They can also be adapted to changing situations in building activity, public and private housing, and ownership or leasing. On the other hand, subsidy programs can influence the development of overall housing production and community building to the extent necessary, particularly in realizing social intentions. Modern housing production is the key for creating new human settlements. Housing is a general problem for every nation as a whole, not just a special problem for certain classes. Subsidy programs give organization and coherence, and direct aid affords opportunities for bridging the gap between economic rents and the actual resources of the lower-income classes and large families. There ought to be ample choice between home ownership or rental, as well as ready means to change residences when a family needs a change.

In many countries housing is so severe a problem that emergency plans are concerned only with providing the dwelling place itself. This is a serious mistake. It completely disregards the principle that a house is only a component of a community, and "community" is the basic unit of society. People need various social activities, a robust political life, effective collective action, and opportunity for developing and exercising public responsibility. Cities and communities must be arranged to foster these essential social institutions. Their adequate provision and servicing is the key to community structure.

In theory this sounds natural, but too often it remains theory and not practice. The number of real towns or even real communities that we create simultaneously is relatively small. Consequently we ought to acknowledge that most of our premises are mistaken. To make a change is essential, but only a change that can affect a significant number of people and the majority of cases will let us accomplish decisive alterations.

Again, all housing and community problems are related. The question of providing housing for low-income groups cannot be answered simply by providing subsidized dwellings. To provide them effectively, policies and programs must go beyond the usual narrow limits; within the usual limits no real solution is possible. It is not possible, for instance, to build cheaply if one is making only a few buildings—it takes a large-scale operation, such as a whole new towns program. And, of course, it is not possible to concentrate on making a "low-cost housing" section in one area, even on a big scale, for that can never be a good community to live in. Thus, low-cost housing (one should really be speaking of hous-

ing for low-income people) is closely connected with the rest of housing production, and that is closely connected with large-scale building, and that is closely connected to such a program as new towns. All of this is possible by bringing dedication and skill to redirect existing means. It is a matter of attitude and intention more than anything else.

Tapiola constitutes one conception among many, one possibility among many. There are numerous other ways to build towns and many more forms. Tapiola is only one test sample of the possibilities, but from it society can judge and learn constructively. Other forms that should be attempted are hill towns, compact towns, seabound towns, valley towns, and so forth. Common sense dictates that all must be tried, for it is necessary to have many different types of cities in the world. The biggest danger is conformity, dullness, and sterility. All towns in the world ought to have their own personalities.

Nor should society wait to build before we are entirely sure of its premises regarding new forms. We should not spend too much time trying to find out what the theoretically "optimal" urban pattern is. Since we need to examine many possible patterns and cannot do so in the abstract, we must build and see as many types as we can think of. We must test real models.

In attempting to follow a model, one has to be very humble at the beginning. One has to be able to admit that one's work may be very much in error. But the only way to progress is by making the best plans possible and by building—one cannot approach problems in theory only. In developing knowledge, criticism is vital, but it must be constructive and must be distinguished from sheer opposition. That can postpone action and be extremely dangerous.

There has been enough research and enough talk; it is time to act. We should not be afraid to make mistakes because step by step we will do the job better and better. We are compelled to start now so as to get into practice and to develop examples. In building Tapiola one problem after another had to be solved. Asuntosäätiö learned by doing, one lesson after another. It did not accomplish the best possible results but did achieve the best that was possible at the time, all things considered. It is this method that permits further progress. We must always aim high and realize the optimal compromises possible.

Urban design is the most demanding form of creative work. It cannot succeed if left in the hands of administrative officials. Administrators and innovative creators need each other and need to understand each other. How little most designers know of what it takes actually to create a city—and how little the administrators know of what the designers can offer and how their skills can be exploited. There ought to be a school to train urban administrative and development experts. There are many fine planners and architects in the world who can design beautiful cities, but there is an extreme shortage of capable administrators able to lead teams, co-ordinate, and organize. Whoever the leader is, whatever his particular professional ability, his first allegiance must be to modern man and his family. The proper use of architects is critically important. Administrators must acknowledge that only those who are creative can do physical planning. In order to make a city with character, we must assemble designers with strong creative talents. If they are not creative, they cannot give personality to a city. Creative work requires freedom, but when plans have to be made, discipline is vital. A further responsiblity of the leader is to consider seriously every single proposal that is suggested.

One thing is already certain. Good planning has proved to be extremely profitable economically and is one of the best investments possible. At this moment exact figures cannot be given, but it can be said that land does not represent the major problem. The obstacles to modern town and community planning are not financial but institutional.

We must reject the prevalent notion that, because towns are growing and will continue to grow, the course and pattern of this growth are immutable. Looking at nature, one can see that growth and development are evident all the time, but one can also see that each type of growth has its limits. The same regularity should apply to mankind. One can already foresee what will happen to the world's population unless limits are placed on its growth. Every big city in the world reveals what will happen if we do not set limits on urban growth. Los Angeles gets its drinking water from a distance of 1,000 miles. Is this sensible? New York, terribly polluted and

getting worse by the day, is well on the way to becoming a slum. Many officials in American cities have good cause to worry, for their taxpayers depart in increasing numbers, and those moving in are mainly poor and asocial. Paris, before World War II the pride and joy of Europe, whose architecture and charming boulevards drew people from all over the world, is deteriorating before our eyes. Charming boulevards with their sidewalk cafes are deluged with terrible traffic, noise, and exhaust fumes. Beautiful buildings, markets, and squares are being overwhelmed. Only the enormous number of cars, chaos, and the cheerless faces of the inhabitants increase. Tourists have also seen this and are beginning to avoid this once delightful city. Paris cannot reform and regain its former position until the traffic in the boulevards and squares has been brought under control and man the pedestrian is again the master.

Consider, too, Stockholm, the capital of one of the most advanced countries in Europe. In an interview in November 1966 with the head of Stockholm's criminal police, Axel Danielsson, it was pointed out that as the city grows, crime of every kind has greatly increased. Danielsson stated that the police are unable to control the situation. They constantly lose ground to crime, which increases daily. During the last ten years, crime almost doubled in the whole country, and 20 percent of it was commited in Stockholm. Assault, theft, robbery, forgery, as well as bank and post office robberies, have increased. The state of the problem is also revealed by the fact that the percentage of crimes solved dropped from 35 to 24. Here we have a report from a country whose standard of living and civilization is one of the highest in Europe. This should give serious food for thought to all who are enthusiastic about ever bigger towns and cities for the sake of size alone.

Surely a modern community is an extremely complex and many-faceted structure. Thus, planning a town is also a many-sided problem, the solution of which must take into consideration dozens of factors. Nevertheless, we continue to witness attempts to solve these planning problems by attending to a few components only, especially to technical and economic components that are usually misunderstood. At the same time, eyes are closed to as many as ten other important factors. And we know the result: a gigantic crisis into which urban civilization has been driven.

No single human being is able to master all the problems of town planning, nor can a single profession—architecture, engineering, planning, economics, psychology, sociology, or medicine. Modern town planning is work for a team, which must be extremely versatile and have members of high intelligence. It should have a leader who is able to make experts cooperate because only then do results begin to appear. The outcome of their work will be towns that are places where it is pleasant to live and easy to work, and where places of work are situated so that valuable free time is not wasted in moving to and from them. This also means that truly economical solutions will be found for the practical problems now confronting us.

Farsighted town planning is one of the best investments society can make. Everyone involved in practical economics should know from experience that erecting a new building is generally cheaper than constant improvising and endless repair of an old one. This holds true for town planning, too. Building a new town is cheaper than repairing an old one. But it is even more important to realize that great mistakes can be made when old, efficiently functioning, and beautiful town units are torn down and new ones built in their stead by piecemeal improvisation. The day may soon dawn when we realize that the growth of a good town has limits that must not be exceeded. This means that if we need new work places and new dwellings and the good old town has no room for them, we must leave the existing town unit in peace and build an entirely new one. Thus we gain two very important advantages: we do not destroy and spoil anything good, valuable, and worth preserving; and we build something new and modern with much less effort and cost.

The problems of urbanization can be solved economically in most countries. To do so, we need town planning based on correct premises, which, however, cannot be realized without regional and overall national planning. Modern town planning can be carried out successfully only if correct planning premises are chosen.

These premises are the following: Man is both the subject and the object of all human enterprise. Industry and economic life exist for man and not vice versa. Traffic must serve man; it must not enslave him. Man is the master; the machine, including the car, is the slave and obedient servant, and nothing else. Our towns must be planned for man and his family, for inhabitants, pedestrians, and consumers. Economic life and industry, as well as traffic, must be organized according to this principle. By discarding incorrect, often damaging, and almost always vastly expensive overconcentration, we save national resources for creating good, pleasant, and biologically healthful surroundings for people—living surroundings, working surroundings, and suitable surroundings to satisfy the requirements of man's increasing free time and cultural needs.

In the last resort, the big problem is not money. If it were, Tapiola would have been created somewhere other than in postwar Finland with its tremendous economic difficulties. The real problem is how to change existing attitudes. Certain fundamentals remain: an idealistic yet practical approach, farsightedness, social and cultural objectives, and administrative skill. Lack of organization and leadership in urban planning is our greatest handicap, not money.

Illustration Credits

Index

Aalto, Alvar
  apartment house
    model, 153
    photos, 23, 153
  Central Helsinki
    model, 50
    plot plan, 51
  Espoo Bay, model, 197
  Finnish Technical Institute
    photos, 51
    plans, 37
    plot plan, 50
  First Neighborhood, 84
  Sunila cellulose factory,
    photo, 46
  Sunila pulp factory, 37
  town planning, 37
Aario, Leo, 165, 166
Adjustment, difficulties of,
  expected, 169
Administration, 164–165
  flexibility in, lack of, 60
Administrative level, re-
  gional, 60
Administrative problems, 1
Aesthetics
  people's sense of, 172
  taste in, lack of, 32
Affluence, relationship of
  housing with, photo,
  100
Agriculture, population en-
  gaged in, 68
Ahola, Pentti
  single house
    floor plan, 138
    photo, 136
  Third Neighborhood, 132,
    133
Ahola concept, model, 135
Ahola houses, courtyard,
  photo, 157
Ahola pattern, site plan, 156
Air routes, map, 71
Alexander I (Tsar:Russia), 28

Allakka apartment, 65
Alterations
  house, charges for, 167–
    168
  plan, policy on, 164
Ambulance service, 171
Amoeba plan, maps, 192,
  203
Amortization, bank loans, 58
Amusement town, 158
Amusements, photos, 174,
  175
Annual mean temperature,
  map, 71
Apartment house, photo,
  171
  five-story, photo, 92
  floor plan, 64, 65
  Itäranta, 153
  Kaskenkaatajantie, 62–63
  Mäntyviita, photo, 61
  prefabricated sections,
    photo, 61
  subsidies for, 59
Apartments
  four-story walk-up, photo,
    145
  Itäranta, photos, 151, 155
  popularity of, 168
  Second Neighborhood,
    floor plan, 130
  two-bedroom, floor plan,
    145
  walk-up, photo, 151
Apathy, overcoming, 10, 11
Arab Village row houses,
  photo, 144
ARAVA, 54
  financing plan, 61, 62–63,
    80
  housing development,
    photos, 64–65
  purpose of, 57
Architectural compatability
  First Neighborhood, 86

Architectural design, 28–53
  coordinating, 83
  in Finland, 28
Architectural detail, photo,
  210
  traditional, 32
Architectural League of New
  York
  Tapiola Exhibit, 188
Architecture
  environmental design, 38
  functionalist, 35
  town planning and, 37
Art of Designing Cities, The,
  32
Artists' studios, photo, 101
Assimilation, of people,
  169–171
Association of Finnish Architects, 57
Asuntosäätiö Housing
  Foundation, 1
  decisions of, challenging,
    169
  make-up of, 78
  nonprofit, 55
  row houses, photo, 152
  and Sevens Towns Plan,
    187
  Tapiola, creation of, 84
  Uusimaa, creation of, 208
Atrium houses, Southern
  Neighborhood, photo,
  156
"Aunty park" (playground),
  photo, 150

Back-to-nature movement,
  17
Baldwin Hills, California, 17
Balance of trade, 68
Banks
  home loans by, 54, 58–59
  as service companies, 171
Basic loans, 58

Basic needs, achievements
  of, 165
Bathroom
  attention to, 168
  mechanical core, 11
Bauer, Catherine, 17
Björnvik Hagalund, plot
  plan, 42
Blomstedt, Aulis
  apartment house, floor plan
    and photos, 65
  First Neighborhood, 84, 87
  Second Neighborhood,
    124
  Third Neighborhood, 133
  weak-link houses
    floor plan, 99
    photos, 96, 97, 98
Bowling alley, Town Center,
  108
Brunila, Birger
  building by, photo, 45
  Käpylä plot plan, 44
Brasilia, Brazil, 18
Building Act (1959), 56
Building coordination, 11
Building costs, 79, 80–82
  and techniques, 58
Building practices
  new towns program, 10
  rural areas, 55
Building registers, 59
Building regulations, 56
Building research, 57
Building restraints, 11
Buildings, harmony of, First
  Neighborhood, 86
Building technology, new
  towns program, 10
Building techniques, costs
  affect, 58
Bus service, 2

Cafe
  Office Tower, 168

rooftop, 180, 181
Camden New Jersey, Yorkshire Village plot plan, 22
Canberra, Australia, 35
plot plan, 40
Capital, owner, 80
Cathedral, *See also* Church
Helsinki, photo, 33
Tampere, photo, 33
Central Association of Tenants, 166
Central Tower, Town Center, 168
model, 111, 112
photo, 115
purpose of, 180
upper floors of, 168
Chain houses
parking, provisions for, photo, 131
photo, 131
site plan, 131
Chandigarh, 18
Chatham Village, Pennsylvania, 17
plot plan and photo, 22
Chaux, 16
Children's park, Itäranta, photo, 150
Children's Town
air view, 136
model, 137
Children
activities, photo, 104
amusement of, photo, 174, 175, 176
amusement town, 158
housing allowances for, 54, 58
play areas, 160
Chmielewski, J., Espoo center plot plan, 66
Choulet, Count of, plot plan by, 19

Church, *See also* Cathedral
photo, 123
Third Neighborhood, 132
Town Center, 108
model, 111, 112
Cinema, 182
Cities, 68
enlarging of, 7, 9
City
Aristotle's definition of, 15
defined, 24
Ciudad Guayana, 18
College, Town Center, 108
Columbia, Maryland, 18
town center, photo, 23
Commercial building companies, 56
Communes, 68
Communities, cooperation among, 60
Community building, 10
Community center, *See also* Town Center
First Neighborhood, 85
Community design, First Neighborhood, 85
Community facilities, First Neighborhood, 85
Community plan, First Neighborhood, 86
Community types, choice of, 10–11
Competitions, on planning level, 56–57
Concert hall, Town Center, 108
"Connurbation," defined, 17
Conservation, 172
Conservatism, overcoming, 180, 215
Constellation form, 26
urban planning, sketch, 27
Construction, rural/urban, 56

Construction problem, new towns, 10
Construction technology, traditional, 57
Consumer preferences, new towns program, 10
Control power, municipal, 164
Cooperation, community, 60
Coordination, levels of, 12
Counties, 68
Courtyard houses, prevalency, 56
Credit, shortage of, 54
Credit policies, 54
Crime rate, Stockholm, 221
Cross-section community, 165
Cultural demands, 1
Cumbernauld, Scotland, 18
aerial photo, 21
plot plan, 21
town center, photo, 22
Cupboard space, 168
Currency unit, 68

Danielsson, Axel, 221
da Vinci, Leonardo, 15
Dåvits estate, purchase of, 187
Decentralization, major cities, 26
Detached houses
Northern Neighborhood, photo, 142
prevalency of, 56
Developing areas, policy on, 60
Design, achievement of, 84
Design procurement, 160
Development, planning for, 59
Developmental entities, First Neighborhood, 87
Developmental goal, 1

Development organizations, 2
Diet of Four Estates, 68
"Dipoli," student union, photo, 51
District center, defined, 1
Down payments required, 82
Dwellings
costs of, 80–82
size of, 58
requirements, 57

Eastern Neighborhood. *See also* First Neighborhood
Helsinki, relationship to, map, 2
population, 158
Economic classes, First Neighborhood, 86
Economic fluctuations, short-range, 10
Economic life, vital to town, 180
Economics, new towns philosophy, 215
Education, 1, 10
Ehrenström, Johan Albert, 28
plot plan, 31
Ehrensvärd, Count Augustin, 28
Ekelund, Hilding, Olympic Village, 37
Ekengren, Bertel, industrial plant, photo, 127
Electricity, supply of, 171
Electric kitchens, 168
Electric power, energy source, 159
Electrified railroad, 208
Elderly, housing allowances for, 54
Elementary school
First Neighborhood, 85

Town Center, model, 111
Energy, electric power as, 159
Engel, Carl Ludwig, 32
  Helsinki Cathedral, photo, 33
Engineering components, coordinating, 83
Engineering costs, municipal, financing, 76–82
England, new towns in, 16, 17
Entertainment, photos, 174, 175
Environment, standard of, 170
Environmental design, architecture and, 38
Environmental misconceptions, photos, 23
Ervi, Aarne
  First Neighborhood, 84
  Second Neighborhood, 124
  swimming pool, photo, 184
  Third Neighborhood, 132, 133
  Town Center, 108, 109, 158
  plot plan and model, 111
Espoo
  industrial centers, plot plan, 4
  planning program, 57
  service companies, 171
  site purchase, 1
  photo, 3
Espoo Bay project, 4
  eastern site, Aalto's model, 197
  plans for, modified, 201
  a reality, 208
  Seven Towns plan, 193

site for, photos, 195
Twin City, plot plan, 196
Espoo Center
  plot plan, 66
  town center, plot plan, 67
  traffic plan, diagram, 67
Exhibition Hall, Town Center, 108
Experience, gained from Tapiola, 12–13
Expressways, 217
Expropriation, power of, new towns, 10

Factories, and housing areas, photo, 46
Family Welfare League
  financial backing by, 73, 77, 78
  Hagalund purchase, 78
Farmland, areas of, 68
Farms, size of, 68
Färsta, Sweden, 17
  row housing, photo, 22
Ferries, map, 71
Financial institutions, new towns program, 10
Financial problems, 1
Financing, 73–80
Financing plans, ARAVA, 61
Finland
  administrative breakdown of, 68
  map, 202
  air routes, map, 71
  architectural and urban design, 28–53
  cities, map, 70
  exports and imports, 68
  ferries, map, 71
  geographical relationship, map, 69
  geography of, 68
  government, 68
  independence of, 28, 35,

68
  mean annual temperature, map, 71
  provinces, map, 70
  railroads, map, 71
  roads, map, 71
Finnish Technical Institute, 2
  Aalto's plans for, 37
  photographs, 51
  plot plan, 50
  student union, photo, 51
Fire prevention code, Helsinki, 32
First Neighborhood, 84–108
  air photo, 90, 92, 102
  center of, at Christmas, photo, 94
  community center, model, 94
  completion of, 85
  map, 84
  model of, 89, 94
  Phase 2, air photo, 102
  plot plan, 101
  plot plan, 88
  social objectives, 86
  Uusimaa site plan, 209
Five-story apartment house, photo, 92
Five-story hilltop houses, photo, 93
Floor areas, 58
Flower beds, maintenance of, 171
Flowers, natural setting, photo, 105
Forest Hills Gardens, New York, 16
Forests, area of, 68
Fountain jets, lighting of, 172
Fountains, photo, 185
Four-story walk-up apartments, Northern Neigh-

borhood, 145
Four-story walk-up housing floor plan, 103
  popularity of, 168
Fourteen-house group, plot plan, 143
France, new towns in, 16, 17
Friluftsstaden, 73
Functionalist architecture, 35

Garages
  common, photo, 131
  Northern Neighborhood, photo, 142
Garden Cities of To-Morrow 16, 17, 32
Garden City
  concept of, 17
  history, 15–18
  Käpylä, plot plan, 44
  new towns concept, 7
  plot plan, 19, 20
Gardens. See also Landscaping
  First Neighborhood, 87
  photo, 97
  Second Neighborhood, 124
  Third Neighborhood, photo, 139
Garden suburb, Kulosaari, plot plan, 40
Geddes, Patrick, 17
Geometric layout, Third Neighborhood, 132
Germany, new towns in, 16
Gesellius, Lindgren, and Saarinen, National Museum, photo, 34
Gottberg, Carl-Johan, 172
Government, Finnish, democratic, 68
Government loans, 80

owner-occupied dwellings, 58

Government subsidies, 54, 55
apartment houses, 59

Grahn, Dr. Arne, 77

Greenbelt, Maryland, 73
photo, 22

Greenbelt towns, 17

Griffin, Walter Burley, Canberra plan, 40

Grocery stores, Third Neighborhood, 133

Ground water, collecting of, photo, 96

Gustavus I (King:Sweden), 28

Gymnasium, Town Center, 108

Hagalund, 35, 77
Family Welfare League finances, 78
plot plan, 75

HAKA, 55
Southern Neighborhood, photo, 155

Hanging roof construction, 159
photo, 127

Harbor facilities, programming, 200

Harbors, planning for, 198

Health, providing for, 216

Health care, new towns program, 10

Heat, supplying, 170, 171

Heating equipment, 57

Heikintori department store, 108, 180, 181
financing, 182
model, 112
photo, 117

Heikintori Mall, photo, 117

Helsinki

architectural design, 32
burdens on, easing, 200
capital city, 28
Cathedral, photo, 33
central section
model, 51
plot plan, 52
decentralization, 26
Eastern Neighborhood, relationship to, map, 2
growth, 32
land increase, 37
metropolitan city, administrative map, 202
Munkkiniemmi-Haaga plot plan, 41
Olympic Village, photos, 48–49
plot plan
about 1800, 30
1917, 31
population, 68
planning for, 37
railroad station, 35
photo, 39
reconstruction (1800), 28
Saarinen's plans, 35, 76
plot plan, 42
Senate Square, photo, 33
Seven Towns Plan, plot plan, 4
size limited, 188
subway system, 37
Suomenlinna fortification, 28, 29
Tapiola, relationship to map, 2, 74
plot plan, 42
Töölö area, plot plan, 36
urbanization of, 32
Uusimaa 2010 plan, 209
Helsinki Area Planning Association, 189

Hertzen, Heikki von, 7, 73

High-income houses, First

Neighborhood, 87

Highways, programming of, 200

High school, model for, 123

Hilltop houses, five-story, photo, 93

Hilversum, Holland, 17

Hobby rooms, financing, 182

Home loans, 54, 80

Holland, new towns program, 17

Homes or Barracks, 73, 74

Hospital service, 171

Hotel
financing, 183
Town Center, 108
model, 111, 112

Hot water, supplying of, 170, 171

House
alterations to, charges for, 167–168
mechanical core, 11
photos, 141
size of, 166

House interiors, photo, 178, 179

House lots, costs of, 79–80

House manager's tariff, 170

House production, since WW1, 54

Housing
condition of, after WW2, 73
coordination of, 59
emergency plans for, 219
financing, 76–82
First Neighborhood, 85
policy on, formulating, 38
Tarjanne design, photo, 34
Third Neighborhood, 132

Housing allowances, 54
for children, 58

Housing areas, and factory,

photo, 46

Housing arrangements, Second Neighborhood, 124

Housing companies
projects completed, chart, 81
purposes of, 55

Housing costs, size and, 58

Housing needs, after WW2, 73, 74

Housing programs, 54–67
national policy, 54–60

Housing site areas, 159

Housing subsidies, 54, 55

Housing Tax Relief Act (1948), 54

Howard, Ebenezer, 16, 17, 35

Hyvinkää, 208

Iharvaara, Lassi, 198

Iltarusko Street, 124

Imports/exports, 68

Independent interests, community building by, 10

Industrial areas, Seven Towns Plan, 193

Industrialization
effect of, 16
Uusimaa, 208
wealth and, 24

Industrialized society, status of, 11

Industrial sectors, plot plan, 4

Industrial technology, new towns program, 8

Industry
decentralization of, 188
labor supply, 159
percentage of population in, 68
plants for, 181
workers' accommodation, 180

Information pavilion, Town
  Center
  model, 111, 112
  photo, 191
Innovation
  new towns program, 10
  shunning of, 32
Insulation, 57
Insurance companies, 171
Insurance rates, 10
Interest rate, 54
Interior finish, 168
Investment capital, shortage
  of, 58
Irvine, California, 18
Itäranta
  apartment, walk-up, photo,
    151
  apartment houses, model,
    153
  children's park, photo, 150
  map, 146, 154
  plot plan, 148, 154
  population, 158
  row houses
    floor plan, 152
    photo, 152
  single-family houses, group
    of, photo, 149
  single-family housing,
    photo, 23
  site plan, 149
  slab apartments, photo,
    155
  wading pool, photo, 150
Itkonen, Uolevi, 172

Jännes, Jussi, 172
Järvi, Jorma
  high school, model, 125
  one-family housing, 81
  secondary school, 132
  Second Neighborhood,
    124
  single-family house

floor plan, 139
  model, 138
  photo, 139
  single houses, photo, 136
  Third Neighborhood, 133
  Town Center, 108
Joint stock building compa-
  nies, 56
Joint stock housing com-
  pany, 170
Jugendstil movement, 32
Jyväskylä, 68

Kajaste, Eino, 83
Käpylä, 73
  buildings in, photo, 45
  garden suburb, 35
  plot plan, 44
Kaskenpaja apartments, floor
  plan and photos, 65
Kazubinski, J., Espoo plot
  plan, 66
Kekkonen, Urho, 208
Kemi, 32
Keskus-Sato, Uusimaa con-
  struction, 208
Keskustorni, 108
Kindergartens, financing,
  182
Kirkkonummi, 208
Kitchens, electric, 168
Kivenlahti, 208
Kivinen, Olli, Third Neigh-
  borhood, 132, 133
Koche, Lieutenant Anders,
  28
Kontiontie area, housing dia-
  gram, 64
Kontiontie Housing Com-
  pany, 81
Koskelo, Heikki
  row houses, photo, 142
  Third Neighborhood, 133
Krupp factory towns, 16
Kruunuhaka, 28

Kulosarri garden suburb
  established, 35
  plot plan, 40
Kuopio, 32, 68
Kuras, K., Espoo plot plan,
  66

Labor force
  distribution of personnel,
    68
  First Neighborhood, 85
  supply, 1, 159, 166
  types represented, 170
Lahti, 68
Lakes, area of, 68
Land costs, 4
Land development, new
  towns program, 10
Land ownership, new towns
  program, 10
Landscaping, 160. See also
  Gardens
  row houses, photo, 101
  Second Neighborhood,
    photo, 129
Landscaping detail, photo,
  211
Landscaping service, 171
Land transfer tax, exemp-
  tions from, 54
Land use
  composition, Tapiola,
    158-159
  controls, 10
  coordination, 59
  laws, 10
  planning for, 59
Leisure demands, 1
Letchworth, 16
  plot plan, 20
Lethargy, overcoming, 10
Languages spoken, 68
Le Vésinet, 16
  photo, 22
  plot plan, 19

Library, Town Center, 108
  model, 111
Lindgren, National Museum,
  photo, 34
Linear form, 26
  urban planning, sketch, 27
Loans
  amortization of, 58
  availability of, 58-59
  bank, 54, 58-59
  government, 58, 80
Local planning, 59
Lohia, 208
Los Angeles, size problem,
  220
Louhenkallio Housing Com-
  pany, 81
Louhentalo Housing Com-
  pany, 81
  capital, 82
Low-cost housing, concen-
  tration on, 219
Lowell, Massachusetts, 16
Low-rise housing, Third
  Neighborhood, 132

MacKaye, Benton, 17
Major alterations, charges
  for, 168
Malmio, Veikko
  "H" houses, photos, 141
  Second Neighborhood,
    124
  Third Neighborhood, 133
  Town Center, 108
Man, individuality of, 1
Mäntyviita, apartment
  house, photo, 61
Marketing, 167-169
Marketing mechanisms, new
  towns project, 10
Mariemont, Ohio, 16
  photo, 22
Maritime activities, planning
  for, 198

Master plans, area of, 56
Mechanical core, of a house, 11
Medium alterations, charges for, 167
Medium-rise apartments, Itäranta, photo, 155
Metropolis
 defined, 24
 forms of
  defined, 26
  diagrams, 27
 size, 25
Meurman, Otto-I., 83
 Hagalund, plot plan, 75
 Käpylä, plot plan, 44
 Tapiola plan, 76, 84
  initial, 37
  modification of, 83
 Town Center, 108, 109
Midwest, America, new towns, 16
Migration, curbing, 188
Miilupolku Housing Company, 81
Miletus, Asia Minor, plot plan, 23, 31
Models, need for, 219–220
Mulhouse, 16
Mumford, Lewis, 17
Municipal engineering costs, 76–82
Municipalities, 68
Munkkiniemmi-Haaga
 plot plan, 41
 Saarinen's plan, 35

National commitment, for new towns, 10
National Housing Board, 55, 57
 loan policy, 59
National Museum, photo, 34
National Pensions Institute

financial backing by, 54–55, 76
National Planning Office, 187
National resources, urban development for, 9
National Resources Planning Board (U.S.), 17
National Romanesque Style, photo, 33, 34
Nationwide planning, 57
Natural environment, proximity to, 1
Neighborhood center, photos, 128, 129
New Lanark, 16
Newspapers, 68, 169
New towns
 areas of needed support, 10
 current concept, 15
 development, survey of, 12
 formation, definition of, 25
 history of, 15–18
 philosophy for, 215–222
 prejudice against, overcoming, 10
 program for, 7
  background survey, 12
  technical knowledge, 8
New Towns Seminar, 199
New York City, a slum, 220
Niemi, Lauri, 171
Noise, problem of, 4
Northern Neighborhood, See Third Neighborhood
Norton, C. McKim, 199
Nyström, Norrmén and Gustaf, Töölö plot plan, 36

Objectives, project, 1
Octopus form, 26
 urban planning sketch, 27
Office Tower. See Central Tower

Old towns, renewal of, 7
Olive, M., plot plan, 19
Olmsted, Frederick Law, 16
 plot plan, 19
Olympic Village, Helsinki
 photos, 48–49
 plans for, 37
One-family houses
 Jarvi type, 81
 prefabricated, photo, 74
Open land, use of, Seven Towns, 190
Operation, 164–165
Otaniemi
 Finnish Technical Institute, 2
 map, 2
 photos, 51
 plot plan, 50
Otsolahden Lämpö Oy, 170
Otsonpesa terrace houses
 floor plan, 106
 photos, 107
Oulu, 68
Owner capital, 80
Owner-occupied dwellings, loans for, 58
Ownership, increase in, 56

Paatelainen, Raili, design by, 51
Pallu, Alphonse, plot plan, 19
Paris, France, deterioration of, 221
Parking areas
 common garages, photo, 131
 costs of, 217
 expanding, 158
 Northern Neighborhood, photo, 142
 plan for, 120–121
 planning for, 37
 Town Center, model, 111

Parks, planning for, 160
Parliament (Finnish), creation of, 68
Paths, photos, 213
Patio houses, Southern Neighborhood
 courtyard, photo, 157
 floor plan, 156
People
 activities of, 212
 amusements, 174, 175
 assimilation of, 169
 entertainment for, 174, 175
 integrating, 170
 Perambulator distance, 133
Pietilä, Reima
 design by, 51
 Third Neighborhood, 132
Pinomaa, K. A., Third Neighborhood, 132
Pinomaa, L.R., Second Neighborhood, 124
Planning, 83–162
 alterations and, 164
 areas of, 56–57
 flexibility in, 85
 levels of, 59
 needs, after WW2, 74
Planning and Building Act, 56
Planning issues, shape and form as, 26
Planning programs, 54–67
 national policy, 54–69
 supervision of, 56
Play areas, 160
Playgrounds, planning of, 160
Play pool, photo, 96
Polar Oy, 182
Police, need for, 160
Political leanings, 167
Pollution, 1
 control of, 159

problem of, 4
Pool, Town Center, 108
Population
concentration of, 189
decentralizing, 215
First Neighborhood, 85
in new towns philosophy,
216–217
optimum numbers, 1, 2
overall, 158
pressure of, easing, 189
Town Center, 109
Population changes, effect
of, 56
Population density, 68,
83–84
Town Center, 109
Population distribution, 68
Population Research Institute, 187
Population Studies, Seven
Towns Plan, 187
Pori, 32, 68
Porkkala Seaside Town, 4
industrial centers, plot plan,
4
maritime activities, 198
photograph, 3
plan modifications, 201
Seven Towns Plan, 193
site, photo, 194
Port Sunlight, 16
Power plant, 171, 181
Prefabricated houses
apartment, photo, 61
popularity of, 168
two-story, photo and floor
plan, 100
Prefabrication, 76
photos, 74
Prefabrication methods, 57
Prejudice, overcoming, 180
215
Primary school, provision
for, 171

Printing plant. See Weilin
and Göös
Private foundation, as builders, advantages, 218
Private property rights, new
towns program, 10
Programming, 83–102
Promenades, Third Neigh-
borhood, 133
Provinces, 68
Provocative town planning,
180–183
Public agencies, as builders,
advantages, 218
Public buildings, planning
for, 37
Public information, 169–
170
Public services,
new towns program, 10
problems of, 4
Public utilities, new towns
problem 10
Pullman, Illinois, 16
plot plan and photo, 22
Puurakenne Oy, prefab-
ricated houses, photo,
74
Puutalo Oy, 132

Radburn, New Jersey, 17,
73
photo, 22
Railroads
electric, 208
map, 71
Railroad station, Helsinki,
35
photo, 39
Rational regional plan
map, 205
photo, 206–207
Recreation
First Neighborhood, 85
problems of, 4

Recreational activities,
photo, 95
Rectilinear layout, Third
Neighborhood, 132
Reflecting pool, town center,
109
Refrigerator space, 168
Regional planning, 59
town planning and, 217
Regional plans, area of, 57
Rent
average cost, 58
income from, 82, 167
Research
contemporary, 57
new town development,
220
Resettlement Act (1936), 54
Resettlement policy, postwar, 60
Residences, types of, photo,
177
Residential community, 15,
16
Restaurant. See also Cafe
Office Tower, 168
photo, 114
rooftop, 180, 181
Restaurant-cafe, First Neigh-
borhood, 85
Reston, Virginia, 18
row housing, photo, 23
town center, photo, 22
Revell, Viljo
apartment house design,
photo, 61
chain houses, photo, 131
First Neighborhood, 84
"Kaskenkaatajantie" apartments, photos and draw-
ings, 62–63
Second Neighborhood,
124
Third Neighborhood, 133
Town Center, 108

Riikonen, Yrjo, 171
Riistapolku Housing Com-
pany, 81
Ring form, 26
urban planning, sketch, 27
Riverside Illinois, 16
plot plan, 19
Roads, 2
coordinating, 83
First Neighborhood, 86, 87
map, 71
Town Center, 109
Roland Park, Maryland, 16
Roof structure, industrial,
photo, 127
Rooftop cafe, photo, 114
Row housing, 73
Itäranta
floor plan, 152
photo, 152
Northern neighborhood,
photos, 142, 144
prevalency of, 56
Second Neighborhood,
photo, 130
Ruusuvuori, Aarno
church design, 132
photo, 123
roof structure, industrial,
photo, 127

Saarinen, Eliel
Canberra plot plan, 40
Helsinki
plans for, 35, 42, 76
railroad station, 35, 39
Munkkiniemmi-Haaga plan,
41
National Museum, photo,
34
SAFA, 57
SAK, 164
Sales, 167–169
Sales Association for Prefab-
ricated Housing, financial

backing, 76
Saltaire, 16
plot plan, 18
Santala, Veikko, 171
SATA, 55
Satellite form, 26
  urban planning, sketch, 27
Save-for-a-Home program,
  55, 166
Savings banks, loans by, 54
Scandinavia, new homes
  program, 17
Schools
  financing, 182
  provision for, 171
  Town Center, 111
Scotland, new towns in, 16
Secondary schools
  provision for, 171
  Third Neighborhood, 132
Second Neighborhood,
  124–125
  air photo, 126
  apartment house, photo,
    23
  atrium houses, photo, 156
  chain houses
    photo and site plan, 131
    landscaping, photo, 129
    map, 124
  neighborhood center,
    photos, 128, 129
  photo, 126
  patio houses
    courtyard, photo, 157
    floor plan, 156
    photo, 23
    plot plan, 123
    population, 158
    row houses, photo, 130
    town houses, photo, 130
Self-interest, overcoming,
  215
Semidetached houses. See
  also Weak-link houses

First Neighborhood, 87
Service companies, 170–
  172
Services, First Neighbor-
  hood, 85
Sewage system, 83
Seven Towns Plan, 187–
  190
  broad concepts, 199
  communities, making up,
    190
  modification of plans, 201
  planning principles, 200
  plot plan, 4
  research on, 188
  sites for, 198
Shadow patterns, photo,
  114
Shape, as planning issue,
  26
Sheet form, 26
  urban planning, sketch, 27
Shopping center
  financing, 182
  First Neighborhood, 85
  photo, 114
  Town Center, 108
  model, 111
Shopping district
  Town Center, 158
Shopping plaza
  model, 118
  photo, 117
  Town Center, model, 112
Short term credit, 54
Shower baths, 168
Single-family house
  Itäranta, photo, 149
  Northern Neighborhood
    floor plan, 138
    model, 138
    photo, 137
Single house, types of, 168
Sipari, Osmo
  Second Neighborhood,

124
Town Center, 108
Siren, Heikki
  floor plan, diagram, 64
  and Siren, Kaiju
    First Neighborhood, 87
    row houses, photo, 130
    terrace houses, floor plan
      and photo, 106, 107
    Third Neighborhood, 133
    Town Center, 108
    town houses, photo, 130
  Second Neighborhood,
    124
  Third Neighborhood, 132
  two-family prefabricated
    houses, 100
Siren, Kaiju. See also Siren,
  Heikki
  floor plan, diagram, 64
  houses, 100
Site details, photo, 173
Site plan
  First Neighborhood, 86
  Uusimaa 2010 area, 209
Site planning, coordination,
  84
Site prices, 76–82
Site selection, problem of, 9
Siutio, 208
Skärsholmen, Sweden, 17
Slums, lack of, 60
Small alterations, charges
  for, 167
Snow covering, 68
Social aims, achievement of,
  7
Social demands, 2
Social fluctuations, short-
  range, 10
Social objectives
  achieving, 9
  First Neighborhood, 86
Söderman, Bror
  row houses, photo, 152

Third Neighborhood, 133
Sonck, Lars
  Kulosaari garden suburb,
    plot plan, 40
  Tampere Cathedral, photo,
    33
  Töölö plot plan, 36
Southwest Coast Consor-
  tium, 208
Sports center, Town Center,
  108
Standardization, 57
Standard of environment,
  170
Standard of living, integrat-
  ing, 170
State Football Pool, financ-
  ing by, 77
State Housing Board, 55
State Institute for Technical
  Research, 57
State Postal Savings Bank
  home loans by, 54
  financial backer, 82
Statistical data, 68–72
Stein, Clarence, 17
Stensvik area, purchase of,
  187
Stockholm
  crime rate, 221
  plot plan, 21
Storage space, floor plan,
  145
Stores
  arrangement of, plot plan,
    116
  Northern Neighborhood,
    photo, 140
Storm drains, coordinating,
  83
Störsvik estate, purchase of,
  187
Streetcar system, 35
Structural plan, defined, 59
Students, percentage of, 68

Subneighborhoods, Second Neighborhood, 124
Subsidy program
  apartment housing, 59
  government, 54, 55, 59
Subway system, Helsinki, 37
Sudenkorento Housing Company, 81
Suhonen, Esko
  four-story walk-up, floor plan, 103
  Third Neighborhood, 132
Sukselainen, V. J., 77
Sunila
  cellulose factory, photos, 46–47
  pulp factory, 37
Suomenlinna fortifications, 28
  photo, 29
Supply companies, 170
Suvanto, Viljo, 171
Suvikumpu, Third Neighborhood, 132
Sweden, new towns program, 17
Swimming pool
  Northern Neighborhood, photo, 143
  photos, 114, 115, 184
  Town Center, 108

Tallin, 28
Tampere, 68, 73
  Cathedral, photo, 33
Tapiola
  background, 15–72
  building of, 73–186
    experience gained from, 12–13
  building costs, 79
  component parts, map, 162
  in context, 8–14

development of, 26
time line, 158
experimental background, 187–211
financing, 76–80
Finnish Technical Institute, plot plan, 50
Helsinki, relationship to map, 2, 74
plot plan, 42
houses, financing, 80–82
key of plan, map-sketch, 6
lessons of, 215–222
map, 163
model, 151
Meurman's plan for, 37, 84
  modifications, 83
  naming of, 169
  in outline, 1–7
  plot plan, 192
  overall development, 161
relevance of, 1–14
site
  prices, 79
  sale of, 79
Tapiola exhibition, 188
Tapiolan Kunnallisteknillinen Huolto Oy, 171
Tampiolan Lämpö Oy, 171, 181
Tampiolan Sahkolaitos Oy, 171
Tampiola Tänään, 169
Tariffs, types of, 170
Tarjanne, Onni, house design, 34
Tausti, Matti, 198
Tavio, Marcus
  apartment buildings, photo, 177
  First Neighborhood, 84
  Second Neighborhood, 124
Taxes

exemptions, 54, 55
problems of, 4
relief from, 54
Temperature, mean annual, map, 71
Tenant screening, 166
Terrace houses
  building costs, 80–82
  floor plan, 106
  popularity of, 168
Theater
  First Neighborhood, 85
  Town Center, 108
  model, 111, 112
Theater groups, 169
Third Neighborhood, 132–133. See also Northern Neighborhood
  Ahola concept, model, 135
  air view, 136
  apartments, two-bedroom, floor plan, 145
  Arab Village row houses, photo, 144
  Children's Town
    air view, 136
    model, 137
  detached houses, photo, 142
  four-story walk-up apartment, photo, 146
  fourteen-house group, plot plan, 143
  garages, photo, 142
  gardens, photo, 139
  "H" houses, photo, 141
  map, 132
  model, 135
  plot plan, 134
  population, 158
  row houses, photos, 142, 144
  single-family house
    floor plan, 138
    model, 138

photo, 136
single house
  floor plan, 139
  model, 138
  photo, 139
  stores, photo, 140
  swimming pool, photo, 142
  town houses, two-story, photo, 144
Three-story walk-up, popularity, 168
Toivonen, Akseli, buildings by, photo, 45
Tomorrow: a Peaceful Path to Real Reform, 16
Töölö
  designs for, 35
  government buildings, 37
  plot plan, 36
Tower houses, popularity of, 168
Town Center, 108–109
  approaches to, photos, 113
  cross-section study, diagram, 120–121
  expansion of, 158
  Helsinki, relationship to, map, 2
  map, 108
  model, 111, 112
  multilevel concept, diagram, 122
  plot plan, 110, 119
  population, 158
  shopping center, photo, 114
  shopping plaza, model, 118
Town council, 164
Town houses
  Northern Neighborhood, photo, 144
  Second Neighborhood, photo, 130

Town plans, area of, 56
Town management, 164
Town planning
  Alvar Aalto's influence, 37
  architecture and, 37
  error in premises of, 215
  farsightedness needed,
    222
  mid-19th century, 32
  problem of, 216
  regional planning and, 217
  teamwork proposition, 221
Towns
  concepts of, 219
  growth limitations, 220
Trade, balance of, 68
Traffic, problems created by,
  217
Traffic costs, 216
Traffic plan, Espoo Center,
  67
Traffic separation, pedes-
    trians/vehicles, 73
Transportation
  coordination of, 59
  problems of, 4
Trees
  conservation of, 172
  shadow patterns, photo,
    114
Turku, 68
  capital city, 28
TVA, building of, 17
Twin City, Espoo Bay, plot
    plan, 196
Two-bedroom apartments,
    floor plan, 145
Two-story houses,
    prefabricated, photos and
    floor plan, 100
  First Neighborhood, 87
  Northern Neighborhood,
    144

Urban design, 28–53

creative work, 220
  in Finland, 28
  problems of, 218
Urban dwellers, basic needs,
  165
Urban form, 24–27
  defined, 25–26
  types of, drawings, 27
Urban growth
  diverting, 9
  limitations on, 220
Urban housing, prevalency
    of, 54
Urbanism, branches of, 8
Urbanity, 24–27
Urbanization, 24–27
  defined, 24
  future patterns, 7
  normal patterns, 7
  past accomplishments, 8
  pattern of, 4, 7
  policy formation, 38
  problems of, solvable, 222
  Uusimaa, 208
Urban renewal, problems of,
  216
Union of Civil Servants, 166
United States, new towns
    program, 16
University of Pennsylvania,
    New Towns Seminar,
    199
University students, percent-
    age of, 68
Utilities, First Neighborhood,
  86
Utopian communities, 74
Utopian philosophers, 15
Uusimaa, 7
  administrative units, map,
    202
  migration flow chart, 201
  models, 200
  in 1968, 208–209
  principles followed, 200

regional plan, map, 205
  target date, 199
  Uusimaa 2010 plan, 7,
    189, 198–201
  acceptance of, 208
  essence of, 200
  First Neighborhood plan,
    209
  Helsinki in, 209
  planning districts, 200
  plot plan, 204
  seven towns proposal, plot
    plan, 5

Vaasa, 32, 68
Välinkangas, Martii, 37
  buildings of, photo, 45
Vällingby, Sweden, 17
  row housing, photo, 22
Vandalism, 160
Vaux, Calvert, plot plan, 19
Viaducts, 217
Viborg, 28

Wading pool
  Itäranta, photo, 150
  photo, 175
Walking distances, plot plan,
  116
Walk-up apartments, four-
    story, floor plan, 103
Waste disposal, program-
    ming of, 200
Wasteland, area of, 68
Water supply
  programming, 200
  Uusimaa, 198
Waterworks, 83
Weak-link houses
  First Neighborhood, 87
  floor plan, 99
  photo, 96, 97, 98
Weilin and Göös printing
    company, 132, 159,
    181

photo, 126
  work areas, photo, 127
Welwyn, 16
  plot plan, 20
Western Neighborhood. See
    Second Neighborhood
Winter season, consideration
    for, 57
Work. See also Labor
  conditions oppressive to,
    215
Workers' towns, 15, 16
World War II, effect of, 54,
    73
Wright, Frank Lloyd, 40
Wright, Henry, 17

Yorkshire Village, New Jer-
    sey, plot plan, 22
Youth centers, financing,
    182
Youth groups, provisions
    for, 169